PRAISE FOR *SMALL BUSINESS SURVIVAL GUIDE*:

"Cliff Ennico's practical, inspirational, and humorous advice is essential for anyone thinking about starting a business or struggling to revitalize one."

—Jane Applegate, noted small business expert

"It IS a jungle out there! Small Busine will help steer you past the problems and challenges of running a small business and lead you to entrepreneurial success."

—Rieva Lesonsky, Editorial Director, *Entrepreneur* Magazine

"This guide has it all; it is a virtual guarantee for your small business success."

—Dr. Laura Schlessinger, internationally syndicated radio talk show host and author of *The Proper Care and Feeding of Husbands*

"We've all heard the statistic, 80 percent (or more) of new businesses fail in the first five years. This book will help put you in the 20 percent (or less) who succeed. There are plenty of books on how to start a company. This one uncovers the threats you face as a small business owner and gives you the strategies that will help make your new (or old) company a success. No business owner should be without this survival guide."

—H. Lee Rust, corporate financ
Company: How to

"Don't let the humor fool you. There
budding entrepreneur can protect h...

—Barbara Weltman, publisher of *Barbara Weltman's Big Ideas for Small Business*

PRAISE FOR *SMALL BUSINESS SURVIVAL GUIDE*:

"I credit much of my success in business to the brilliance of Cliff Ennico. Early in my career he taught me what NOT to do. I listened closely to his wise counsel and avoided costly mistakes as a result. This book covers all that and much more. It's on the 'must read' list for all my clients."

—Jane Pollak, business coach, small business expert, and author of *Soul Proprietor: 101 Lessons from a Lifestyle Entrepreneur*

"Anyone who owns a small business or is considering becoming an entrepreneur must read this comprehensive, no-B.S. guide immediately. It will educate you on topics you are afraid to face—yet should be dealing with. It's invaluable!"

—Julie Jansen, author of *I Don't Know What I Want, But I Know It's Not This*

"There are thousands of small-business books, but Cliff Ennico's approach is unique; his Small Business Survival Guide will help you look at business in a completely different way. It's well written and humorous, providing an easy way to learn how to avoid the many pitfalls of working for yourself and to ultimately succeed in your business."

—Peter Kent, the author of *The Complete Idiot's Guide to the Internet* and *Search Engine Optimization for Dummies*

SMALL **BUSINESS** **SURVIVAL** GUIDE

Starting, Protecting, and Securing Your Business for Long-Term Success

CLIFF ENNICO

ADAMS MEDIA
Avon, Massachusetts

DEDICATION

To my wife Dolores: here, there, and everywhere, forever and ever . . .

Published by
Adams Media, an F+W Publications Company
57 Littlefield Street, Avon, MA 02322. U.S.A.
www.adamsmedia.com

ISBN: 1-59337-406-2

Printed in the United States of America.

J I H G F E D C B A

Library of Congress Cataloging-in-Publication Data

Ennico, Clifford R.
Small business survival guide / Cliff Ennico.
p. cm.
Includes index.
ISBN 1-59337-406-2
1. Small business--Management. I. Title.

HD62.7.E56 2005
658.02'2--dc22

2005016014

CONTENTS

INTRODUCTION

THE BEST OF TIMES (AND THE WORST OF TIMES) FOR RUNNING YOUR OWN BUSINESS

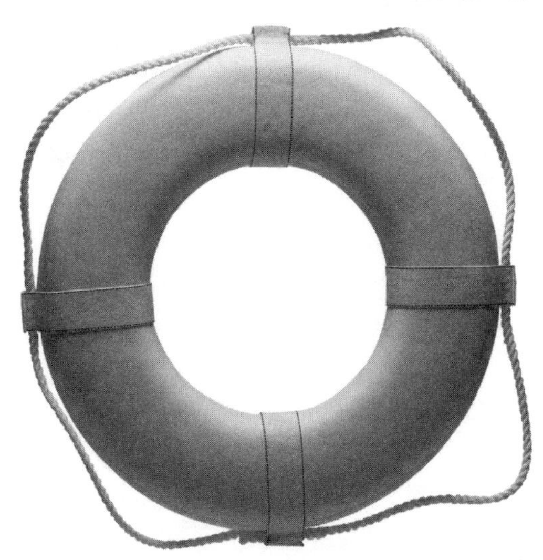

Millions of Americans dream of starting their own businesses, for a number of reasons:

- » They are tired of working for someone else and want to "be their own boss."
- » They are worried that they won't have a job or that their future income will not support the lifestyle to which they have become accustomed.
- » They think they can make a lot more money than they do working for a company or boss.
- » They think they will have a lot more leisure time or have a more flexible schedule, when they are running the show.
- » They know, deep in their hearts, that they can do a better job serving their marketplace than the people they work with (or for).
- » They are tired of doing something day after day that does not make use of their superior education or creative skills.

The U.S. Small Business Administration (SBA) estimates that there are 30 million self-employed people in the United States. I personally would estimate that another 60 million—fully one-quarter of the American population—wish they were. We live today in a nation of armchair entrepreneurs.

Yet, the very same SBA—the government agency that wants everyone to start their own businesses and has set up some excellent programs to help first-time entrepreneurs get their plans off the ground—tells us that more than 80 percent of all small businesses fail within the first five years of operation. Since the SBA bases its information only on published reports and statistics, the actual failure rate may be significantly higher than 80 percent.

With apologies to Charles Dickens, there has never been a better time in human history to own your own business,

and there has never been a worse time in human history to own your own business.

Why the Best of Times?

A number of socioeconomic trends, some of them unique in history, have combined over the past twenty years to create a "perfect storm" of entrepreneurial fervor and have made the dawning years of the twenty-first century a perfect time to start a business.

ADVANTAGE #1: Rapid Advances in Technology

Remember how it was to work in 1985? If your work involved any type of paper-shuffling (and what work doesn't?), you did it on a manual or electric typewriter, with carbon paper. Actually, you didn't do it yourself; you had to pay a secretary or assistant to do it.

Boy, how times have changed. The computer, software, telecom, and wireless communications revolutions of the last twenty years have totally changed the way we live and work. Our machines—desktops, laptops, notebook and pocket PCs, cell phones, PDAs, Blackberrys, Treos, GPS and iPod devices, and more—enable us to do things that people could only have dreamed of doing in 1985. The technology is incredibly cheap and getting cheaper every year.

ADVANTAGE #2: A Surplus of Education and Information

The Baby Boom generation and its rearguard in Generations X and Y are probably the most educated people in American, if not human, history. The average corporate executive in the United States today has at least four years of college, a couple

of years of graduate school, and a welter of "continuing education" programs under his or her belt. Thanks to the wealth of information available on the Internet and a proliferation of self-help books, seminars, and audio and video resources, you can become an expert in anything, anytime, in a matter of months if not weeks, for an extremely affordable cost.

ADVANTAGE #3: The Legacy of the 1960s

As a member of the Woodstock generation, I like to credit the antiestablishment bias of that decade as a leading cause of today's boom in business ownership. The generations that came of age in the 1960s, '70s, and '80s were taught, consciously or not, to challenge authority and institutions of all types and to be highly skeptical of any point of view that threatened individual freedom and autonomy. The idea of working for "the man" is as uncomfortable for today's young people as it was to denizens of Haight-Ashbury in San Francisco circa 1967.

Why the Worst of Times?

Have you ever noticed that the thing you really love about someone is precisely the same thing that drives you crazy? It's the same here—the very socioeconomic trends and developments that have fostered an entrepreneurial culture in the United States in the new millennium are also the things that make this "the worst of times" to start or run a business.

PROBLEM #1: Rapid Advances in Technology

In the 1980s, you needed thousands of employees to run a billion dollar corporation. Today you can run the same

corporation with fewer than 100 employees if you have the right information systems, computer hardware, and software. And corporate employers have taken note: Hundreds of thousands, if not millions, of corporate employees have seen their jobs lost in "downsizings"—not to other companies, divisions, or business units, but rather to the little white box that used to sit on their desk.

Remember back in the 1980s when people said all this new technology would give us more time to live our lives by eliminating unnecessary or repetitive tasks from the workplace? What they forgot to consider was Parkinson's Law—that work expands, not contracts, to fill the allotted amount of time. If technology makes it possible to work twenty-four hours a day, seven days a week, you will. If technology makes it possible for clients and customers to contact you twenty-four hours a day, seven days a week and disrupt whatever you may be doing for other customers or clients, they will. If technology makes it possible to turn documents around in an hour that used to take two days, your clients will demand one-hour turnaround. Look around you during your morning and evening commutes and count the number of "cell phone slaves" who can't break free of the office for even a moment.

PROBLEM #2: A Surplus of Education and Information

You really have to wonder sometimes if there isn't a little too much education and information out there. All of us are looking for the "best deal" when it comes to buying goods and services. We only pay more than the "best deal" when the cost of getting a better deal is prohibitive.

Today, with only a few clicks of your computer mouse, you can access information in "real time" (that means right now) about all possible deals. For example, you now can find out:

» Exactly the lowest fares on a flight from New York to Miami next Thursday (www.travelocity.com)
» The exact amount your car dealership pays for each option on a new 2005 Toyota Camry (www.carprices.com)

If you don't like any of the prices out there for something you want, you can tell the world how much you want to pay for something and let suppliers from around the world bid for your business (www.priceline.com).

By doing away with those quaint "inefficiencies" (such as personal service) that made our parents and grandparents sometimes happy to pay more than rock-bottom prices for things, our world of perfect, instant information drives customers to people who offer the lowest prices. Almost always, those people aren't small businesses. Think about that the next time you buy a cheap knockoff from China, pick up your groceries from Wal-Mart or CostCo, or make a $20 bid for a new digital camera on eBay.

PROBLEM #3: The Legacy of the 1960s

Far be it from me to criticize the values of the Woodstock generation, yet I sometimes wonder whether the pendulum between "respect for authority and institutions" and "respect for individual freedom and autonomy" hasn't swung just a little too far in the latter direction. We live in a world in which everyone has unlimited and unfettered choices, rights, and opinions and the right to express them at all times without the shaping force of institutions and cultural norms to limit the available options to a manageable number. As an example, our parents had only "mass media" that was broadcast from on high; someone else determined the content of the message, and they had to listen to it, like it or not. We

have the Internet and other self-driven media that enable us to choose (or "Google") information based on our personal preferences; increasingly, we determine the content of the message and what we will and will not listen to.

As a result, individuals become more and more isolated from their communities and from points of view that differ from their own. They spend less time looking outside themselves for the interests and values they share in common with their neighbors and spend more time looking inside themselves and developing their own individual, personal, unique points of view, interests, and systems of values. Businesses are then compelled to tailor their products more and more to the specific needs of individual consumers—a very difficult and expensive thing for small businesses to do with their limited resources. It may be easy for a small business to develop a new type of breakfast cereal, but will it have the ability to quickly roll out the fifteen different flavors and varieties that consumers will almost immediately demand?

You May Not Have a Choice

In the final analysis, it doesn't really matter whether it's the "best of times" or the "worst of times" to run your business. For at some point, every one of us is going to have to at least think about running our own business, either full-time or part-time.

Many of your parents worked for large corporations, but you cannot count on them any longer to provide you with a lifetime living. Today's computer technology has eliminated the need for large corporate staffs. Our global economy often forces corporations to hire people overseas who can work for a fraction of the salaries and benefits their American competitors need. If only Americans can do the job, many companies prefer

to hire them as independent contractors who will not receive benefits, health insurance, or other employee "perks." If only American employees can do the job, many companies will feel pressure to squeeze every last drop of "productivity" (translation: the most work for the least compensation) out of them. In today's volatile economy, even the most "employee friendly" company can be taken over by a competitor, lose a key product due to obsolescence, or fail due to poor management. All of which are outside of your control.

When it comes to earning a living, sooner or later you will be on your own. At some point, you will find yourself in a situation, at least temporarily, where you must rely on your own efforts to generate the income you need. You can best do this by owning and running your own business.

So What's Keeping You from Getting Started?

Yes, it takes a lot of courage to start a business. Yes, there will be some sleepless nights. But I have worked with more than 5,000 people who have done it and succeeded, and believe me, a lot of them weren't as smart as you must be. (After all, you're reading this book, aren't you?)

Entrepreneurs are the new American heroes and heroines. What politicians were in the 1960s, rock musicians were in the 1970s, investment bankers were in the 1980s, and software entrepreneurs were in the 1990s, people giving up the corporate rat race and starting their own businesses are in the first years of the new millennium.

What prevents even more people from getting out on their own is cold, naked fear. I have been teaching a management course for first-time entrepreneurs for almost twenty years, and I recognized early on that the biggest fear most people experience when they contemplate starting a business is the fear that someone else will steal their success. Among the most frequently asked questions at my programs are:

» How can I prevent someone from stealing my idea (or my business name)?
» How can I prevent the government from taking everything I've earned in taxes? (The United States taxes self-employed people at the highest rates in the world.)
» How can I prevent my business creditors from getting their hands on my personal assets?
» How can I make sure the business stays in my hands if my spouse and I divorce?
» How can I make sure the business doesn't end up in the hands of my ne'er-do-well kids if something happens to me?
» How can I make sure my lawyers and accountants don't screw me over?

The fear that someone else—an undeserving someone else—will come along at the right time and claim the glory and wealth that you have worked years to build up can often overwhelm even experienced entrepreneurs.

While it is true that in entrepreneurship "only the paranoid survive," this particular fear is not unjustified. Many successful small businesses have been wiped off the face of the Earth because of events such as these:

» The founder dies and his or her heirs are forced to sell the business in order to pay federal and state death taxes.
» A powerful competitor steals the entrepreneur's ideas and mass-produces a cheaper, less efficient product.
» Sloppy management gives a creditor an opportunity to seize both the entrepreneur's business and personal assets.

- » Inexperienced entrepreneurs who don't recognize their own limitations fail to hand over the keys to professional managers at the right time.
- » Inexperienced entrepreneurs hand over the keys to their business too soon and end up as middle managers of the companies they founded.
- » Lawyers and other professional advisors in a position of trust abuse their positions to gain unjustified stakes in their clients' companies.

What This Book Is About

The *Small Business Survival Guide* identifies a number of people and other things (like old age) that pose a challenge to your business, your assets, your ideas, and your success, and it offers time-tested, successful, and affordable strategies for coping with each of them.

Each chapter begins with a description of a particular person or thing you will encounter when running a small business and the challenges to your safety and security that person or thing may present. We will not refer to them as "enemies" in this book, since some of them (such as your spouse, your successor, or even yourself) may actually like you and certainly don't view themselves as such. They are not conscious of the threat they pose to you, and they will be offended if you suggest openly that they do. Often, the biggest challenge in dealing with such people is finding a way to protect yourself from them without tipping your hand that you view them as a threat to your business success!

After describing the challenges posed to your business, each chapter then either provides a strategy or solution for dealing with them or gives examples of actual entrepreneurs who have faced this challenge and found a creative way to conquer it.

Note: All stories recounted in this book actually happened, but some names and irrelevant facts have been changed to preserve the privacy of the subject.

What This Book Is Not

Let's get this out of the way right now: This book is not—emphatically not—a "legal guide" for small business owners. My goal is not to teach you about the law, what it says, or how it affects your business. If that's what you want, there are at least 1,000 books out there that can help you.

Rather, my goal is to teach you the defensive strategies you will need to protect your business against a host of natural and sometimes surprising challenges in the environment. We have some discussion of legal tactics—after all, any business strategy, offensive or defensive, must be legal, or else it will do you more harm than good. But I have learned the hard way that business owners don't really want to know much about the law—what they want is answers, solutions, a plan, and/or a direction.

In my career, I have had the privilege of working with more than 5,000 small business owners and entrepreneurs with the sole objective of keeping the wolves away from their doors. I cannot say that none of them have ever been sued or that an especially creative and aggressive wolf (with incredibly deep pockets) isn't occasionally able to huff and puff and blow down all the defenses we have worked so hard to build. It's a relatively rare occurrence, however, and most of my clients tell me they sleep a lot better at night because of the techniques, tactics, and strategies described in this book.

The *Small Business Survival Guide* is designed to help you anticipate threats before they become too dangerous, counter threats before your opponent obtains the advantage, and sleep

better and more securely at night while building a successful small business. If you want to become a legal expert, go to law school.

A Word about Corporations, Partnerships, and LLCs

Small businesses can be organized in a number of ways. There are sole proprietorships, general partnerships, limited partnerships, corporations, Subchapter S corporations, limited liability companies (LLCs), and limited liability partnerships (LLPs), among others. For a concise description of the different ways of organizing a small business and the pros and cons of each, please download a free outline I hand out at my small business seminars across the country called "Demystifying the Business Organization" from my Web site at www.cliffennico.com. It should answer most of your questions about the advantages and disadvantages of each form of organization and will spare us having to delve into that complicated topic in the text of each chapter, where much more important work will be done.

The strategies, tactics, and techniques described in this book are not dependent upon the particular form your small business takes—whether you are an LLC, an LLP, or a corporation, they will work equally well.

A Word about Legal Forms and "Boilerplate" Provisions

I have included a number of legal forms, clauses, and other documents in an Appendix at the end of the book to illustrate some of the more important points that may be unfamiliar to

you. These forms and a number of additional forms referred to in the text are available on my Web site at www.cliffennico.com. When in doubt, I chose limited liability company (LLC) forms and documents, since the LLC is probably the most popular form for organizing small businesses these days. If you are a corporation or other type of organization, these forms can be easily adapted to fit your business—just be sure an attorney or other competent professional does the job!

The forms, clauses, and provisions that appear in this book and on the Web site are for general educational and information use only, and they are not—I repeat, not—to be reprinted, copied, or used as an inexpensive substitute for competent legal, tax, financial, or accounting advice.

In the almost twenty-five years I have been practicing law, I have never once—not once—been able to just take a preprinted legal form, fill in the client's name, and hand it to the client as a finished product without making at least some additions, deletions, or changes to it. Every client and every business situation is just a little bit different, and one size definitely does not fit all when it comes to legal documents. Each one has to be custom-tailored to a specific situation.

Also, state laws contain widely varying requirements pertaining to the use of forms such as these. What works in New York often will not work in California and vice versa. This is especially true of the agreements between spouses that are referred to in Chapter 7 of this book. New York is an "equitable distribution" state when it comes to divorce, and California is a "community property" state, where things are done a lot differently. Using a New York form in California is guaranteed to lead to lots of trouble.

Before using any of the forms in this book, you absolutely must have them reviewed by an attorney licensed to practice law in your state. If he or she recommends another form or another solution, use that one instead of the form in

this book. Doing otherwise may be harmful to your business, and if you are dealing with any of the situations I'm describing in this book, you don't want to make things any worse than they already are.

Acknowledgments

This book would not have happened without a number of key players, the most important of whom are:

My editor Jill Alexander, who believed in this project before a lot of other folks did;

My agent Rick Broadhead, for his patience and persistence;

My mentor and good friend Jane Applegate, who first pointed out the need for this book; and

My wife Dolores, for being quite simply the most wonderful human being on Earth.

Cliff Ennico

CHAPTER 1

YOUR COMPETITORS: THEY'RE OUT THERE

It downright amazes me when a new client or a student in one of my entrepreneurial classes looks me straight in the eye and says this: "My product or service is so unique that it really has no competition."

Poor fools—they're lying to themselves, and they don't even know it.

Every business has competition. It's just that some competitors are harder to find than others. Whoever says "I have no competition" simply has not done their homework. There's plenty of competition in any business, and thank goodness! If you didn't have competition, you would have a tough time selling your stuff. Who is adventurous enough to buy something they can't compare to other existing products or services?

One of the biggest reasons business owners lose out to their competition is that they fail to look long and hard enough to identify their competitors and develop counteractive strategies. By waiting until your competitors become urgent and immediate threats, you limit your ability to defend against them.

Your Markets Define Your Competitors

A lot of business owners would define their competition as follows: "people who make or sell the same kind of stuff that I do." Nothing could be further from the truth, and if we're going to develop strategies for dealing with competitors, we first have to recognize who these people really are.

Take, for example, two publishers. The first publishes books, audiotapes, and other "self-help" information products designed to help lawyers, paralegals, and other legal professionals manage their careers better. They produce books with titles such as *How to Make Partner at a Law Firm, Which Legal Specialty Is Right for You?*, and *Big Firm, Small Firm,*

Corporate Legal Department: Finding the Right Fit for Your Legal Career.

The second publishes books, audiotapes, and other "self-help" information products designed to help doctors, nurses, and other medical professionals manage their careers better. They produce books with titles such as *How to Make Partner in a Medical Practice, Which Medical Specialty Is Right for You?*, and *Private Practice, Hospital, or Corporate Medical Department: Finding the Right Fit for Your Medical Career.*

At first look, it seems the two publishers would be arch-competitors. After all, they are both serving the professional career information marketplace, and they publish books with almost identical titles on the same or similar subjects.

Yet, do they really compete?

If the "legal" publishing company doubles its sales to lawyers, paralegals, and other legal professionals, does it hurt the "medical" publishing company's sales one bit? The answer is clearly "no." Lawyers and doctors are in entirely separate marketplaces and have no earthly reason to buy career information that is directed to the other market.

Your competitors are not necessarily people that are doing the "same things" you are doing. They are the people that are going after the same markets you are trying to reach, whether their products and services are similar or dissimilar to yours.

Specifically, competitors come in four flavors or varieties: direct, indirect, actual, and potential competitors. Let's take a look at each one.

Direct Versus Indirect Competitors

Competitors can be either "direct" or "indirect." A direct competitor is a person or firm that:

- Has targeted the same customers or clients you have targeted for your business;
- Is trying to arouse the same fears and passions you are trying to arouse in your customers or clients, in order to persuade them to buy;
- Is offering a product or service that is the same as or similar to the product or service you are offering to your customers.

Say, for example, that I was to write a book for lawyers on "how to interview for a legal job." Shortly after the book is published, you write a book called *The Real Secrets of Interviewing for a Legal Job or Why Cliff Ennico Is Full of It.* Clearly, I won't like the idea of your writing a competing book (especially with that subtitle!), but unless you steal my words and try to infringe my copyrights (more on that in Chapter 3), there is absolutely nothing I can do about it. The First Amendment to the U.S. Constitution gives you the right to write a book on any topic you want, and if the market is big enough, there can be sixty or seventy different books in print dealing with the subject of how to interview for a legal job.

Here's an easier example. If I decide to open a pizza parlor on Main Street in my hometown, the six pizza parlors that already have located on Main Street are my "direct" competitors.

Direct competitors are fairly easy to spot. But we can't stop there. We have to consider "indirect" competitors as well.

An indirect competitor is a person or firm that:

- Has targeted the same customers or clients you have targeted for your business;
- Is trying to arouse the same fears and passions you are trying to arouse in your customers or clients, in order to persuade them to buy;

» Is offering a product or service that is significantly different than the product or service you are offering to your customers.

So, in the case of my book on how to interview for a legal job, a company that publishes an audio guide on how to interview for a legal job, a lawyer that teaches an adult education class for lawyers on interviewing skills, and an interactive Web site showing the right and wrong way to interview for a legal job would all be indirect competitors to my book. Anything that teaches lawyers and other legal professionals how to interview for a legal job (but that is something other than a book) is an indirect competitor of mine and must be taken seriously.

Here's an example. If I decide to open a pizza parlor on Main Street in my hometown, the six pizza parlors that are already located on Main Street would be my direct competitors, but the Chinese takeout place across the street may well be an "indirect" competitor. While his menu is almost entirely different from mine, we are both in the market of serving local customers who want a quick lunch of ethnic food.

Actual Versus Potential Competitors

We have now identified direct and indirect competitors, but we're not done yet. Direct and indirect competitors can be either "actual" or "potential" competitors.

An actual competitor is one that is actually in business today. If I open a pizza parlor on Main Street in my hometown and there are six pizza parlors in business on Main Street when I open my doors, each of those six pizza parlors are my "actual" competitors. They are in business right here and now, and I will have to work hard to grab market share away from them.

Actual competitors are fairly easy to spot.

Potential competitors are the competitors of the future. A competitor who is not already in business, but who could easily get into my market with a reasonable amount of effort and (here's the key) wipe me out because of his superior economies of scale, is a potential competitor.

So, in my Main Street pizza parlor example, if I learn that a neighbor of mine is thinking about opening a pizza parlor down the street from mine, that neighbor becomes a potential competitor of mine. I'm not likely to lose much sleep over that, though, since my neighbor is likely to be a "Mom and Pop" operation just like mine, will have resources that are just as limited as mine, and will face the same challenges grabbing market share that I will. In fact, I've got a clear competitive advantage over my neighbor just by virtue of having opened my doors long before he opened his and establishing my reputation locally. My neighbor will have an uphill fight.

But now, let's say I find out that Olive Garden, Pasta Fair, Bertucci's, or one of the other large franchised Italian restaurant chains is planning to open a chain restaurant right across the street from my pizza parlor. I'm a lot more worried now, aren't I? Because a major chain can offer a much broader menu, a full wine list, and other amenities to its customers that I can only dream of providing.

The point here is that you not be worried about all potential competitors. The ones you should lose sleep over are the ones with resources that can wipe you off the map.

I can actually think of one person who could, at one time, have said that he "had no competition." His name was Marc Andreesen, and he was the founder of Netscape, the company that developed the first commercially viable Internet browser in the mid-1990s. In 1995, if you surfed the Internet at all, you used Netscape as your Internet browser. There were one or two "Mom and Pop" software products that competed with

Netscape, but Netscape easily owned 98 percent or more of the marketplace for Internet browsers.

Andreesen honestly believed he owned and would continue to own the marketplace for Internet browsers. But who was lurking out there, sitting on top of Mount Rainier in Washington State with a pile of money that enabled him to get into any marketplace he pleased? Bill Gates of Microsoft, of course. He cast his hungry eyes on the Internet browser market and saw that it was good. In 1996, Microsoft launched its own Internet browser, Internet Explorer. In 1998, Microsoft had 40 percent of the browser market. By 2000, Microsoft had 80 percent of the browser market. Today, if you use Netscape as your primary Internet browser, you are a member of a tiny minority.

Ask yourself this: "If I knock the cover off the ball and establish a nationwide market for my products and services, what big companies are out there that could get into my market and wipe me out?" If you don't like the answer, don't launch the product or service.

The Competitor Grid

Now that we've identified the four types of competitor, let's consider the following grid.

	DIRECT	INDIRECT
EXISTING		
POTENTIAL		

This grid has boxes for filling in the types of competitors who are both direct and existing, or indirect and potential, and so on. Who goes into each of these boxes?

Your "Direct and Existing" competitors are the ones we'll call your enemies. These are the competitors that pose the biggest threats to your business and must be dealt with aggressively and creatively as a high priority.

Your "Indirect and Existing" competitors are products and services (and the companies that make them) that your customers can use as substitutes for your products and services.

Your "Direct and Potential" competitors are large-scale companies or franchise chains—let's call them big-time players—that can provide a wider variety of products and services at much lower cost, with national or regional advertising behind them, and with other economies of scale that you cannot match on a small business budget.

Your "Indirect and Potential" competitors are products and services (and the companies that make them) that will make your products and services obsolete. These competitors might be called innovators—even though in many cases they may not be that innovative themselves, but simply followers of the newest developments. For example, a manufacturer of buggy whips and other equine-related accessories in the year 1920 had to look not only at other buggy whip manufacturers, but also at companies making these newfangled gadgets called "automobiles" as the competitors of the future. In the same way, any publisher of self-help books today has to look at the Internet and Web sites targeting its market, as the indirect competitors of the future.

So now that we've identified the four types of competitors, let's fill in the grid.

	DIRECT	INDIRECT
EXISTING	Enemies	Substitutes
POTENTIAL	Big-time Players	Innovators

Consider the pizza parlor example given earlier. If you are opening a new neighborhood pizza parlor, an enemy would be another independent pizza place a few blocks away. A substitute would be a Chinese restaurant across the street, and a big-time player would be Pizza Hut (unless they already have a store in your area, in which case they are an enemy). An innovator might be someone who establishes an online pizza ordering system—or perhaps even someone who invents something that people like to eat more than pizza (though this seems hard to imagine, doesn't it?).

When a Competitor Becomes an Opportunity

If the last box of the competitive grid—the Innovators box—is becoming an obsession to the point where you are beginning to view it as your most significant source of competitors, I would recommend that you consider it as much of an opportunity as a threat. If a new technology is looming on the horizon, perhaps what life is telling you is that you should be the company that steps into the breach first and establish yourself firmly as "the company to beat" in that category before anyone else thinks to do it. In other words, perhaps the best strategy for dealing with potential obsolescence is to jump into that box yourself with both feet, become your own biggest competitor, and gradually force your "obsolete" products (and those of your less innovative and courageous competitors) out of business so you can own the entire category for a while, at least until other competitors come along who take the technology to the next level.

It may sound strange, but there are times in business when you must compete with yourself. This is especially true in times (like ours) of rapid technological change. Innovations that render your existing products and services obsolete are, of

course, a threat to your business. But those same innovations can also give you the opportunity of a lifetime, if, that is, you are courageous enough to embrace the "new order" and drive your old products or services out of business before anyone else gets the chance.

Four Ways to Leapfrog the Competition

The best strategy for beating a determined competition is to outflank or "leapfrog" it—take your business to another level that attracts business away from the competitor and forces it to play "catch-up."

There are many ways to leapfrog the competition, of course, but here are four common (and very effective) strategies.

STRATEGY #1: Focus on a Niche

Find a niche in your marketplace that's not being served adequately by your existing competition and saturate it before your competition catches on that it's even there.

Years ago, I spent my undergraduate years in a small college town in northern New England. At the time, there were only two places in town where you could get a sandwich at times when the college dining hall was closed—a "deli" run by the college arts center and a small off-campus establishment run by a local family. Clearly, the on-campus location had a real advantage in that it was more conveniently located (for students, anyway)—it was right near the post office boxes where students received mail from home, and you could count on the quality, since the sandwiches were made by off-duty college dining hall staff.

Still, there was a big problem—the college-run "deli" closed at 5 P.M. each day. The off-campus sandwich shop was open later but involved a long walk from campus. One day, the owners of the off-campus shop came up with a brilliant idea. At the end of each day, the shop always had a couple of dozen sandwiches left over, which they were in the habit of throwing out before they became stale. Why not hire a couple of college students to pick up the leftover sandwiches at the end of each day and bring them to students in their dormitories late at night, when nothing (and I mean nothing) in town was open and the students were desperate for something to munch on? The shop could charge more for the sandwiches (after all, they were the "only game in town" at 10 P.M.), and it would let the student "salespeople" keep 20 percent of the gross as their compensation.

The shop decided to do it. They hired two students to make the late-night dormitory runs, and within days the sound of "sandwich man, sandwich man" echoed over the intercoms in each dormitory between 9 P.M. and 11 P.M. every night. The response was so overwhelming that the sandwich shop had to double its production every day to fulfill the "after-hours" demand, and sales at the college-run deli declined approximately 30 to 40 percent, that is, until the campus "deli" managers got wise to the scheme and extended their hours to 10 P.M. each night.

STRATEGY #2: Get Intellectual Property Protection

If you develop a product or service that can be patented, trademarked, or copyrighted, you can obtain a "legal monopoly" on that product or service for a period of years, giving you the exclusive rights to make money on that product or service and (more importantly) to exclude others from making or selling what is protected by your patent, trademark, or copyright for a period of years.

In the late 1990s, U.S. courts extended the patent protection traditionally available to inventions to "business processes," including such infamous examples as Amazon.com's "one-click-shopping" feature and Priceline.com's "name your own price" feature. The exact extent to which business processes can be patented is still being fought out in the courts, but if you've come up with a new way of offering a product or service (especially online) that makes your customers' lives a lot easier, you should definitely talk to a patent lawyer before launching it in a public forum where everyone can see it and copy it.

STRATEGY #3: Get Big Fast

If your products and services are being marketed to more than just a narrow niche of customers and there's no possibility of getting a patent or trademark on your product or service, there is a strategy for crushing the competition that can be very effective, at least for the short term. I call it "GBF," for "get big fast."

The classic example of this strategy is Snapple beverages. In the early 1990s, when Snapple virtually invented the "natural" beverage category, it realized that there was little to prevent the major beverage companies from developing competing products, as there was nothing in the beverage formula that could be protected via patents. So, Snapple launched a major marketing and distribution campaign and got their products into delis, sandwich shops, and other nonsupermarket venues before the major beverage companies knew what hit them. For awhile, whenever you wanted a natural beverage, you ordered a Snapple.

The problem with a "get big fast" strategy is that it seldom can be sustained over the long run. In Snapple's case, once Coca-Cola and Pepsi realized the potential of the "natural" beverage market, they quickly launched their own lines of competing product, leveraging their exhaustive national and international distribution chains. We all know the story. Rather than compete head-on with Coca-Cola and Pepsi, the founders of Snapple decided that "discretion was the better part of valor" and sold the company to Quaker Oats, a company with little or no experience in the beverage industry.

STRATEGY #4: Take Things to the Next Level

There are at least twenty pizza parlors in my hometown. Last year, a new pizza parlor opened in a ramshackle cinderblock building on the edge of town that used to be a seedy gun shop. It's located behind a gas station at the end of a gravel path, whose entrance is difficult to find, and has only three parking spaces in front of the building, which are used by the parlor's employees. It almost seems as if the pizza parlor is discouraging customers, which in a way it is.

The pizza parlor's gimmick is "We deliver all orders, no matter how small, for two dollars; every pizza is half off the listed price during our first year in business, and all soda is free." The poor location has the advantage of being extremely low-rent, which keeps costs to a minimum, while the three parking spaces are for the parlor's delivery people, who race around twenty-four hours a day, seven days a week, delivering pizza to college students and families all over town. It explains the bizarre location; they don't want customers coming there because then they would have to buy tables and have a waitstaff. They want to come to you, and they don't mind paying high prices for gas (did you wonder why they located right behind a gas station? I smell a deal there, don't you?). Guess who's mopping up the sauce in the pizza business in my hometown these days? Just about every person driving around town has had a "near miss" with one of this parlor's

delivery cars, which prominently advertise the parlor's toll-free phone number and "half off pizza, free soda" policy. A couple of family-owned pizza parlors in town have gone out of business because they can't match the new parlor's business model, while others are copying the new parlor's strategy, hiring elderly retirees as drivers who hand out discount coupons for the "sit-down" restaurant so people will go there and try some of the higher-margin Italian dishes.

Now, I have to say I've tried the new parlor's pizza, and it's okay—not any better, not any worse than what a lot of other pizza parlors in town sell. The new parlor isn't competing by building a "better pizza." What they did instead is change the way people in the town look at pizza—no longer is it something you go to get. Rather, it comes to you. Would you rather pack your screaming kids into your SUV, drive along crowded roads to the parlor, unpack the kids, wait in line, buy the pizza, repack the kids into the SUV, drive back home, and microwave the pizza because it's gotten cold in the time you took to get it? Would you be willing to pay a couple of extra bucks to have it home delivered? Of course, you would.

Keeping the Giant Corporation at Bay

One of the most common "famous last words" of an entrepreneur whose company is dying is: "I thought my customers would be loyal to me." Ask any small-town hardware store owner who's had to go one-on-one with Wal-Mart or Home Depot if this is true. While not totally dead, customer and brand loyalties are not as strong as they used to be. People won't buy products from you just because they've bought from you for thirty years. If a new competitor is offering a better price to your customers and the cost of changing vendors isn't all that great (for example, if the cheaper competitor is located in a faraway, hard-to-reach place, people may continue to pay your higher prices for the convenience of a shorter trip), people will switch to the competitor in a heartbeat. By all means provide better service than your competitors, but don't count on it. You should also offer the lowest prices around and keep your costs even lower.

Years ago, we had a music store in town that came up with a unique gimmick—the owner invested serious money in several "listening booths" where patrons could listen to new CDs on private headsets. That way, the owner reasoned, customers could learn about new music and new artists they hadn't heard of before and would be more willing to pay $18 a CD for unfamiliar music once they had listened to it. The owner went a step further. Realizing that most CD customers detested having to struggle to open the CD's shrink-wrap packaging, he hired a couple of high school students to remove the packaging from each new CD that came into the store, so that when a customer bought a CD, it was ready to play. Because of the higher costs the owner incurred for these "value-added" services, he felt he had to charge full price for the CDs, figuring that customers would be happy to pay it for the extra service, expertise, and hand-holding that he and his well-trained staff (all professional musicians) would provide.

So what do you think was the reaction? Surprise, surprise—everyone in town frequented his store and used the "listening booths" to learn more about new CDs and recording artists, but then they would walk down the street to a major chain music and record store where they could buy the same CD for 20 to 30 percent off the list price. When I asked one customer why he wasn't buying his CDs directly from the store where he had first listened to them, his response was "I would if they would leave the CD in its original packaging, but they take the shrink-wrap off all their CDs, and I'm worried that I'm

paying full price for a CD that's been used and listened to by a dozen other people." Oops!

By the way, have you visited your local major chain music store lately? They all have private headsets where you can scan a CD's "bar code" and listen to it without having to break the shrink-wrap. My friend the CD store owner had the right idea; he was just ahead of his time by a few years.

To fight a "big box" competitor, you've got to do some serious information gathering and Internet research to find out the competitor's "Achilles' heel." What do customers in other areas where the bigger store is located complain about the most? Perhaps a particular line of merchandise that the bigger store doesn't stock in quantity because they don't think there's enough market interest? Perhaps an inconvenient location in the heart of a rundown industrial district that suburban soccer moms are reluctant to visit in their SUVs? Whatever the "big box" retailer's weakness, be sure to counter it in your business and be sure your competitive advantage is featured prominently in your advertising.

When You Can't Beat the Competition

Sometimes you can't beat the competition. What then?

Once upon a time, there was a small family-owned bookstore in a small town in the rural Midwest—one of three small bookstores supported by a community of perhaps 10,000 readers. One day, a construction crew broke down on a strip mall in the downtown business district, and the bookstore owner heard a rumor that the "anchor tenant" for the mall would be one of the major bookstore chains. Doing a little research and learning that two of the other largest bookstore chains had stores in nearby towns and probably wouldn't want to "cannibalize" their sales by opening a new store in town, the owner reasoned that the mystery tenant had to be the third major bookstore chain, which didn't have any stores whatsoever in that part of the state.

So the owner picked up the phone, called the president of the third chain, confirmed that indeed the chain had eyes on the "strip mall" site, and then made the president an offer he couldn't refuse: "Look, my family has been running a bookstore in this town for nearly thirty years. We know that with your heavily discounted prices and huge selection of books, there's no way we're going to compete with you, and we'll have to close our doors. But here's an idea. Why don't you hire me and my wife as the managers of your new bookstore here in town? Everybody in town knows us, and when they see us greeting customers at the door, they'll feel at home and you'll have a much easier time getting the store up and running than if you staff it with a bunch of strangers. You know the book business a lot better than we do, but we know this town and its readers a lot better than anyone else around. We'll run the business your way, and take your training program for store managers. What do you think?"

Sure enough, the chain hired them, they shut down their family bookstore, and they went to work a few weeks later at the new chain bookstore's "grand opening." The other two bookstores in town also closed their doors, but sadly, the chain store didn't have enough available jobs to accommodate their owners.

The moral of the story: If you can't beat 'em, join 'em. You may not make as much money, but the benefits are great, there's at least some job security, and you're still a "player" in the business you love.

CHAPTER 2

YOUR CREDITORS: YOUR WORST NIGHTMARE

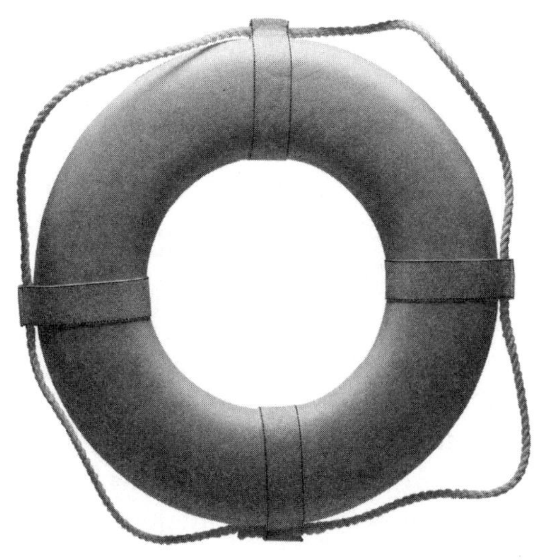

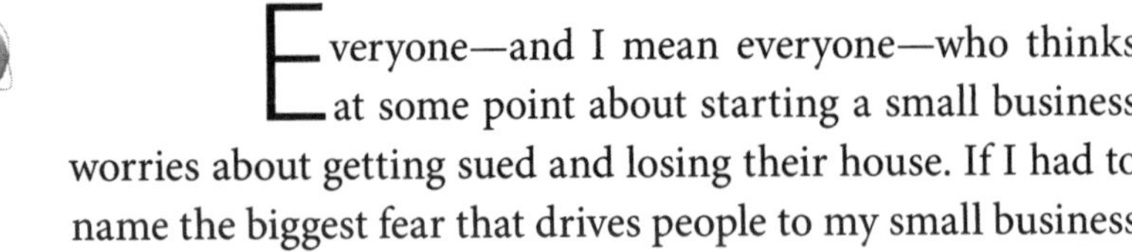

Everyone—and I mean everyone—who thinks at some point about starting a small business worries about getting sued and losing their house. If I had to name the biggest fear that drives people to my small business management seminars around the country, this is it.

We are all willing to take risks, up to a point. But few of us are willing to risk all of our personal assets on a business venture that may or may not work out. Drawing a line between "personal assets" and "business assets" is an obsession for many entrepreneurs. This chapter will focus on some common strategies for separating the two.

The Two Types of Creditors

First, we have to identify the creditors your business might deal with. Basically, there are two types: the "financial creditor" and the "judgment creditor."

The financial creditor is anyone who lends money to your business. A bank, a rich relative who lends you $100,000 in start-up capital, the U.S. Small Business Administration, your American Express Gold Card or "Optima" credit line, and your Aunt Irma who is willing to "give" you some money to get started provided you "pay it back as soon as you can" are all financial creditors. Financial creditors are not accidental—you sign written agreements with them, providing for the repayment of their loan with interest at a commercially acceptable rate.

Financial creditors are relatively easy to deal with (with the exception of Aunt Irma) because they won't lend anything to you unless they're 100 percent satisfied you have the wherewithal to pay it back on time and with interest. Also, because their loan is evidenced by written documents, you can tell exactly where you stand with them, and you know that as long as you make payments on time, you won't have any problem with them.

The second type of creditor is a judgment creditor. This is someone you owe money to because you did something bad (or neglected to do something good), and they've gotten a judge to agree that you owe them money. Anyone who slips, falls, and injures themselves in your store, anyone you hit with your car while on company business, and anyone who claims you bought something from them and didn't pay them on time are all judgment creditors.

Judgment creditors are extremely difficult to deal with because, unlike financial creditors, you cannot plan for them in advance. They can (and usually do) crop up by accident, and there's no telling exactly how much you owe them until a judge renders his or her verdict and hands you the bill. More than the reality of financial creditors, it is the prospect of judgment creditors who keep my clients awake at night.

Piercing the Business Veil

If you are a sole proprietor or a partner in a partnership, everything you own is on the line when you go to work each day.

When you have a corporation or limited liability company (LLC), however, you are attempting to place a wall or "veil" between your personal assets and your business assets. If I form a corporation, for example, and put $100,000 of my money into the corporation as start-up capital, my $100,000 is at risk, but everything else—my house, my stamp collection, my autographed photo of Mortimer Snerd—is safe from the grubby paws of my corporation's creditors.

Having said that, though, there are circumstances under which my corporation's creditors can "pierce the corporate veil" and reach my personal assets, even though I properly formed my corporation or LLC.

How to Avoid "Veil Piercers"

When you form a corporation or LLC, there is a certain discipline you must adopt to make sure that nobody can "pierce the corporate veil"—basically, blow away your business entity and reach your personal assets.

The biggest mistake people make when they form corporations and LLCs is that they don't use them once they're set up. When it comes to protection against liability, as in all of life, if you don't "use" your corporation or LLC, you will lose it; it won't be there to protect you if someone tries to sue you and pierce the veil to get at your personal assets.

There are three disciplines you should adopt to discourage would-be veil piercers.

DISCIPLINE #1: Use Your Business Name Everywhere

If you have a corporation or LLC, make sure the company name (including the abbreviations "Inc.," "Corp.," or "LLC") appears on all of your business cards, stationery, letterhead, marketing brochures, Web site, and any other piece of paper or HTML page with which your customers, suppliers, and other business relationships come in contact. I see a lot of people set up a company with the name "Cliff Ennico LLC," but their business cards still say "Cliff Ennico." Not only is that bad form, but also if someone sues you, they may be able to argue that "I didn't know anything about any LLC; I did business with Cliff Ennico, and that's all I know." Don't help them make that argument.

DISCIPLINE #2: Maintain a Separate Checking Account

If you have a corporation or LLC, you should obtain a separate tax ID number for the business and open a separate business checking account for the corporation or LLC. The name of the corporation or LLC should appear prominently on each check, and your customers should be encouraged to make their checks out to "Cliff Ennico LLC" and not to "Cliff Ennico." Never, ever, ever let people write checks to "Cliff Ennico" and then deposit them in your personal checking account. Doing so will open wide the doors to a "veil piercer."

DISCIPLINE #3: Use a "Signature Block"

When signing letters, documents, agreements, or indeed anything on behalf of your corporation or LLC, use a "signature block," as follows:

FLIBBERTIGIBBET ENTERPRISES, LLC

By: ______________________

Cliff Ennico, its President

This makes it clear that the addressee is not doing business with "Cliff Ennico," but rather "Flibbertigibbet Enterprises, LLC," which is acting through its president, who just happens to be Cliff Ennico but is acting in his representative capacity, not his personal capacity.

One more thing: when you endorse checks on the back, use a signature block as well. In other words, when people make checks payable to "Flibbertigibbet Enterprises, LLC," you should endorse the check on the back using the preceding signature block. If this is a hassle, have your bank (or a local UPS Store or MailBoxes Etc.) prepare a rubber stamp with all of the "signature block" information, stamp the back of each check with the rubber stamp, and sign your name on the signature line. For only $10 or $15, it's cheap insurance and will help ensure that "veil piercers" won't be able to accuse you of doing business in your individual capacity.

A Word About "Trade Names"

Every once in awhile, even though you have a corporation or LLC, you want to do business using a different name. So, you may be "Flibbertigibbet Enterprises, LLC" doing business as "Flibbertigibbet Antiques." In that case, you should file a Trade Name Certificate (see the form called "Certification of Adoption of Trade Name" at www.cliffennico.com) with the Town Clerk or County Clerk in the municipality where you will maintain your business office and make sure the Certificate indicates clearly that it is the corporation or LLC, not you personally, that is claiming the "trade name."

Often, when you file a Trade Name Certificate, you get sloppy and file it in your individual name—"Cliff Ennico, d/b/a Flibbertigibbet Antiques." If you do that, an unscrupulous attorney for a disgruntled creditor may use that filing to argue that "Flibbertigibbet Antiques" is a separate line of business from Flibbertigibbet Enterprises, LLC. If the judge buys that, your personal assets will be on the hook even though you had a perfectly functioning LLC when you did business with this bozo.

Should You Transfer Assets to Your Spouse?

I'm frequently asked if transferring all of your personal assets to your spouse or a close relative before starting up your business will protect you against creditors.

The short answer is as follows: Transferring personal assets to a spouse or relative before you start a business should protect those assets against subsequent claims by creditors. If you wait until a creditor starts asserting a claim and then transfer the assets into your spouse's or relative's name, it won't work. Why? Because the law allows courts to "set aside"—essentially call back—transfers that were made for "less than adequate consideration" and "for the sole purpose of hindering or delaying a creditor." So, if you wait until the "wolf is at the door" and then start transferring assets madly out of your name, the courts won't buy it. But if you transfer the assets before doing business with the creditor, it probably will work. The judge in such a case would say, in effect, "too bad for the creditor who did business with someone without checking to see if they had sufficient assets to pay their debts."

When you decide to transfer assets into a spouse's or relative's name, it's very important that you observe the legal formalities. If your state requires a deed to transfer ownership of a personal residence, have the deed recorded in the local land records so that it's a matter of public record. If your state requires you to prepare a new Certificate of Title to transfer a motor vehicle, then stand in line at the local Department of Motor Vehicles (DMV) office and make sure the Certificate is legally transferred to your spouse. A Quitclaim Deed (which you can find at www.cliffennico.com) is a typical form of Quitclaim Deed by which you would transfer your ownership of a personal residence to your spouse. Most real estate attorneys I know would charge you only a one-hour fee (plus recording and filing fees) to prepare and file such a document.

One caution, however. When you transfer all of your assets into the name of a spouse or relative, you are putting a lot of pressure on the relationship. If you and your spouse subsequently divorce or if your spouse suddenly and unexpectedly dies, your home, your car, and other transferred assets all legally belong to the spouse and become part of his or her estate. You may not only find yourself divorced or widowed, but you may also be homeless and auto-less as well. You should consider that very carefully before transferring any assets into your spouse's or a relative's name. I never want to see any of

my clients on an interstate highway exit ramp holding a cardboard sign saying "Will Run a Small Business for Food."

Liability and Other Insurance

Every new small business should look into insurance as a defense against liability. Of course, having a drop-dead policy of life insurance won't prevent you from getting sued, but it's a lot more tempting for your creditor to go after a big, fat, juicy insurance policy than it is to place a lien on your house or safe deposit box.

I always advise clients to buy as much liability insurance protection as they can afford. But there's more to insurance than liability, and it's worth mentioning here.

I owe my insurance agent an awful lot. When I was first setting up my solo law practice, I asked my agent to get quotes for my professional liability insurance policy (also known as "malpractice insurance"), since I wasn't about to go into practice uninsured. My insurance agent did put that together for me, but she did me an additional favor that actually saved my life.

When I visited my agent to sign the paperwork for the malpractice insurance, she said, "Cliff, once you finish with the malpractice insurance, there are a couple of other things we need to talk about. I'm not going to let you out of this office today until you've signed up for disability insurance." At first, I couldn't believe my ears—disability insurance? That's pretty expensive coverage, and it's mostly for people who work with their hands and bodies. A lawyer works with his or her mind—as long as I have functioning brain cells and a personal computer within easy reach, I can practice law. Why does someone like me need disability coverage?

Her answer still rings in my ears: "Look, it isn't just a question of your mind. You are going to be working out of your home. You've made up your mind not to see clients in your home, which is very smart, but that means you're going to be relying heavily upon your car to get you to clients' offices, local diners, your local MailBoxes Etc. outlet, and wherever else you will be meeting your clients. Let's say you have an accident and break your right foot. You can't drive a car without a right foot—think about that when you drive home tonight. If anything ever happened to your right foot, you could still work on your computer all right, but you wouldn't be able to see anyone unless they came to you. You would be out of business."

Frankly, I thought my insurance agent was out of her mind, but I did let her talk me into buying disability coverage. Boy, I am so glad I did.

Because . . . on Bastille Day (July 14) in 2001, I was out barbecuing in the backyard in my stocking feet. In our backyard, we have a rock ledge with a rock wall on top of it; the top of the wall comes up to about chest-high. A couple of my neighbor's kids were playing touch football and crashed into the rock wall, knocking loose a couple of stones. In my stocking feet, I went over to the rock wall to put the stones back on top of the wall.

Well, the rock wall must have been loosening up over the years; when I tried to replace the first stone the kids had knocked off the top, the entire rock wall collapsed on me. I tried to jump out of the way, but a big 25-pound rock came crashing down on my right foot, smashing it to smithereens. Just like that. One minute I'm out in the backyard grilling hamburgers, and the next minute I'm dragging myself across the backyard and screaming in pain for my wife to drive me to the emergency room.

I was in a cast for nearly six months, during which time I couldn't drive. You can't drive without a right foot—has anyone ever told you that?

I am thankful that my pushy insurance agent talked me into that disability policy. Without it, I would have had to shut down my law practice and go back to a corporate job. With the proceeds, I hired one of my neighbor's kids (the older brother of the kids that knocked the stones off my rock wall—their father owed me at least that much) to drive me around and help me with my paperwork so I could keep up with my clients' deadlines. He enjoyed the job so much he's now applying to law school. Go figure.

A Word from a Police Lieutenant

Can you ever really keep yourself from getting sued?

Years ago, I was the police reporter for a daily newspaper. Every year, I had to interview a member of the city police force and write a story about "ways to keep your home from being burglarized." One year, I interviewed a grizzled old detective lieutenant who had been on the force for forty years and was getting ready to retire. When I asked him for tips on how to keep burglars at bay, he gave me the following extremely candid answer:

"You know, you really can't prevent your home from being burglarized. Today's burglars have highly sophisticated tools that are better than anything we have in the police force, and they can break into just about anyone's home if they're motivated enough. What people can do is slow the burglar down.

"Like any other professional, a burglar wants to make his job as easy as possible, and he doesn't want to take unnecessary risks. He knows that his chances of getting caught and going to jail double or triple each minute he spends in your house. Once he's in your house, he has to find the stuff he knows he can sell and get out of your house in ten minutes or less. If he thinks he's going to have a tough time doing that, he will stay away from your house.

"So by all means put double locks on all your doors, put bars on your windows, get yourself a vicious barking dog, and clear away all the shrubs around your house so the burglar has no place to hide. If a burglar sees you've done all of that, he will see your house as a high risk, and he will stay away. Just recognize that anything you do is not 100 percent foolproof. If you've got the *Mona Lisa* in your living room and the burglar knows that, he may be motivated enough to take the risk and try to break through all of your defenses."

This is excellent advice for homeowners, but what does it have to do with protecting yourself against lawsuits? Everything. When you run a business, you cannot ever be 100 percent certain that you won't be sued, but there are lots of things you can do to make yourself an unattractive target. You can form a corporation or LLC and make sure your customers and suppliers know that they are dealing with it. You can get lots of liability insurance so a disgruntled plaintiff will go after that rather than your house and other personal assets. You can make your customers sign waivers in which you disclaim legal responsibility for anything bad that might happen to them. You can deed your house and other important assets over to your spouse, provided your spouse is not involved in your business.

Even if you do all these things, you are not 100 percent judgment proof. If someone is angry enough, rich enough, and spiteful enough to bring a lawsuit just to make your life miserable, you're in trouble. But most folks (or their lawyers) will look at your defenses, realize that it isn't worth "throwing good money after bad" to sue you, and will go away. They will go away mad, of course. They may try to hurt you in other ways (such as badmouthing your business to everyone they know or posting "negative feedback" on eBay), but they probably will not sue you.

So, to answer your question, as soon as you have the cash to do so, get extra liability insurance, form a corporation or LLC for your business, and make sure each piece of paper is signed by the corporation or LLC so your clients and suppliers know they are not dealing with you personally. The other thing you can do is to treat your clients so well and respond to their problems so promptly that no one ever thinks to sue you in the first place.

CHAPTER 3

COPYCATS: "THE SINCEREST FORM OF FLATTERY"

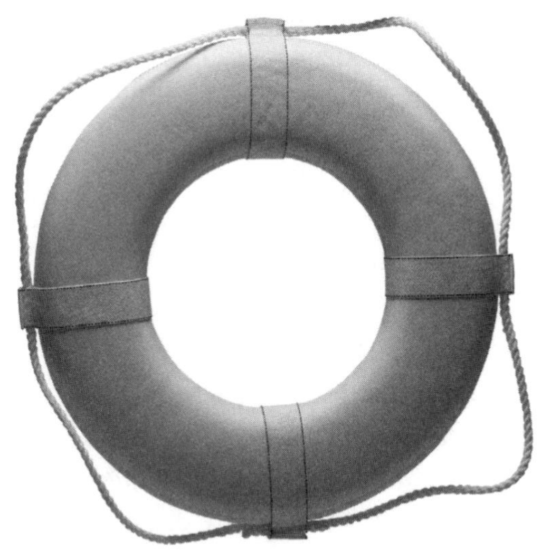

If your business idea is any good at all, two things are guaranteed to happen: (1) people will start competing with you, in the hope that there's room for more than one player in your marketplace, and (2) people will start knocking off your products and services, in the hope they can get away with it. Chapter 1 contains strategies for dealing with your competitors; now it's time to deal with the copycats.

As my grandmother used to say, "Imitation is the sincerest form of flattery." Copycats, in their own way, are paying you one of the highest compliments in the business world. Yeah, Grandma, just as long as it's legal . . .

Your Most Valuable Assets

These days, a company's most valuable assets (at least in the United States) aren't its manufacturing facilities, its equipment, its inventory, or even its people. More often than not, a company's most valuable assets are the ideas, concepts, and "intellectual property" that it has originated that underlie and form the basis for its products and services.

The problem with ideas, of course, is that they're easy to steal. We live in a society that promotes the free exchange of ideas on the theory that no innovation is ever truly 100 percent original. The early personal computers of the 1980s were advertised as revolutionary new devices designed to totally transform your home and make you more productive than you ever could be without one. But let's take a look at those early personal computers. What did they look like (and, to some extent, still do)?

Basically, they're a television set connected to a typewriter keyboard by a telephone cord, aren't they?

Of course, personal computers do a lot more than any of those items individually could do; my point is that when the early PC manufacturers designed their early products they fell back on designs and models that were already commonplace items in the home. I'm sure this was done partly to make the PC less threatening to its early users. But can you imagine what the early PC manufacturers would have had to go through if individuals or companies "owned" the idea of a telephone cord, or a television set, or a typewriter keyboard? The PC would have been impossible to build and launch, unless the "owners" of those three technologies banded together in a joint venture and went into the PC business.

The "free exchange of ideas" is a sacred principle in our democracy, but it can be a pain in the neck when you've come up with a new idea and want a fair shot at launching it in the marketplace before anyone else thinks of it.

How Do I Protect My Idea?

Legally, you can't. You can protect the physical manifestation of an idea or concept—the design or the technology. With a patent, you obtain a "legal monopoly" on the design and rendering of a particular invention that embodies your idea. With a trademark, you obtain a "legal monopoly" on a name or mark you will use to identify your goods and services in the marketplace. With a copyright, you obtain a "legal monopoly" on a particular arrangement of words in the English language (such as this book).

The idea itself, though, cannot be legally protected. It is public information, legally available to all who have occasionally had original thoughts, and there's little you can do about that. Except, of course, don't talk about it to anyone who hasn't signed a nondisclosure agreement or NDA with you (see the following).

The Nondisclosure Agreement (NDA)

The nondisclosure agreement or NDA, also called a confidentiality agreement, is designed to make sure that a "strategic partner" or other company you do business with on a regular basis treats any confidential information they learn from you with respect. Likewise, you should agree that the partner's information will be kept confidential as well.

There are two working parts to an NDA—a "nondisclosure" clause and a "use" clause. The nondisclosure clause prohibits your partner from disclosing to anyone other than you any information about your business that they may learn in the course of your business relationship. The use clause, actually the more important clause, prohibits your partner from taking advantage of your confidential information in his or her own business. A sneaky game that some people play is to give you an NDA to sign that has the standard nondisclosure clause but omits the use clause—so your "partner" can freely steal information from you as long as he doesn't technically disclose the information to someone else. When asked to sign an NDA, you need to be sure both clauses appear in the agreement.

When using NDAs, it's extremely important to define precisely what you mean by "confidential information." Anything you view as a "trade secret" (such as your secret recipe for your knock- 'em-dead baked goods) should, of course, be included. Your list of customers, suppliers, and other business relationships should also be treated as confidential and covered by the NDA. I always recommend including a catch-all phrase for "any and all information, of any type or nature whatsoever, that the Disclosing Party designates, either verbally or in writing, as 'confidential' at the time of disclosure." That way, if you're not sure if the law will treat information as confidential or not, you can make it confidential by saying so before you disclose it. Of course, I would recommend you do this in writing.

You have to use a little common sense, though, when defining confidential information. The copy of today's *Wall Street Journal* sitting on your receptionist's desk is not confidential, nor is the fact that you have a genuine Picasso painting hanging in your office lobby. While many NDAs I see try to protect "ideas" and "concepts" that the other person develops as a result of looking at your confidential information, in practice it is very difficult to protect those, since the other party can always claim they "independently developed" the idea or concept without using your confidential information. What you can do is put in a clause that includes in the definition of confidential information "any idea or concept developed by personnel of the Receiving Party who, as evidenced by either Disclosing Party's or Receiving Party's internal records, had access to the Confidential Information of the Disclosing Party, within three years of the date of this Agreement." That should at least make your "alliance partner" think twice before using your proprietary data to invent a better mousetrap of their own.

See the Mutual Nondisclosure Agreement at www.cliffennico.com for an example of a "mutual" nondisclosure agreement in which two companies entering into a joint venture each agree to keep confidential any information they may learn from the other party in the course of the relationship.

Your Independent Contractors Have Rights

Let's say you started a software company a number of years ago. You're not really a programmer, and so you hire a student from the local community college to do the coding and

bug testing of your initial release. He ends up writing a good portion of the software. You paid him well for his work, and you made it clear in a written agreement that he was clearly an "independent contractor" and not your employee for tax purposes. (This issue is discussed in detail in Chapter 5.) It's been years since he worked for you. Your company has grown and you're getting ready for your first venture-capital financing. Suddenly at some time in the future, you get a letter from this individual's lawyer (he's no longer a kid now) demanding 10 percent of your company's stock. When you tell the lawyer you never promised the kid a piece of the action, the lawyer says you would have to give him something since he holds the copyright on a significant piece of your software product, and it will be really embarrassing for you if the venture capitalists find out about that. It sounds like extortion, doesn't it? Is there anything you can do about it?

Up until 1989, you would have been completely in the right. If you paid someone to work for you, you owned what they produced, whether or not the person was technically your employee. In 1989, the U.S. Supreme Court turned the entire world of copyright on its head by ruling that artists, writers, composers, and other creative types who contribute to a literary, artistic, or other copyrightable work (such as a software program), even if they are paid for their services, own the copyright to their contribution unless they either (1) are employees of the person who paid them or (2) assign their copyright in writing to the person who paid them. In other words, an employee who is paid to contribute to a literary or artistic creation (software programs are included in this category) "sells" his contribution to his employer without having any sort of written agreement, but an independent contractor only does so if he assigns his rights to his client or customer in writing.

As for the student, while you did the right thing by getting him to agree in writing that he is not an employee (saving yourself the trouble of having to withhold federal and state income and payroll taxes), you should also have required him to sign an "assignment of rights" clause (see the Assignment of Rights Clause available at www.cliffennico.com) granting you "all right, title, and interest" to the software code, technical documentation, and other work product he delivered to you. While the lawyer's implied threat to tell the venture capitalists that you do not own all the rights to your software product is probably a form of extortion, sadly, it is perfectly legal extortion, and you will probably have to give the kid something in exchange for an "assignment of rights" agreement at this late date.

How Do I Protect My Name?

What's in a name? For a small business, especially one that provides services rather than goods, the answer may be "everything." For businesses that have few tangible assets, the goodwill associated with a name that is well respected in the marketplace may constitute the entire value of the business. So protecting a unique or special name becomes an important task for the owner of a new business.

In talking to small business owners in my seminars and in my law practice, I find there are several myths and misconceptions about the right way to protect a business name legally. Here's how to simplify the process so that you don't waste time, energy, and money on a process that takes you away from the day-to-day running of your business.

Filing a "Trade Name Certificate"

If you are doing business using a name other than the one that appears on your birth certificate, you are doing business under a "trade name." In some states, it's called a

"fictitious name" or a "DBA," which stands for "Doing Business As." For example, if I open a law office and call myself "Clifford R. Ennico, Attorney at Law," I am not using a trade name. Why? Because if you look at my birth certificate this is exactly what you will see (not the "Attorney at Law" part, of course, but certainly "Clifford R. Ennico"). But let's say that I take out an ad in a local business newspaper and call myself "Cliff: The Legal Guy." That's a trade name. Even if I call my business something more subdued, such as "Ennico & Associates" or "Cliff Ennico Legal Consultants," I am using a trade name, even though the trade name incorporates a part or an abbreviated version of my real name. If it's anything other than my full legal name, "Clifford R. Ennico," it's a trade name.

There are two things you need to know about trade names. The first is that if you are doing business under a trade name, you must register the name with the town or city clerk's office of each town and city in which you have an office location. This includes Post Office Box addresses and "rented mailbox" locations. For example, if your home office is based in Yonkers, New York, but you maintain a post office box in Stamford, Connecticut, for your Connecticut customers, you will need to register your trade name in both Yonkers and Stamford. The fact that you service customers throughout the tristate New York, New Jersey, and Connecticut area does not require you to register your trade name in every city, town, and village within that area. You register only where you have a physical location such as an office or mailing address.

You do not need to hire an attorney to register your trade name. You simply visit the town or city clerk's office, ask for a "trade name certificate," fill it out, sign it, and pay a filing fee, which is usually between $5 and $15. The "trade name certificate" is not a legal document. It is merely a notice which reads something like the following: "I, Clifford R. Ennico, residing at thus-and-such an address, am doing business at thus-and-such an address using the trade name 'Cliff: The Legal Guy.'"

The second thing you need to know about trade name certificates is that they do not offer you any legal protection for your trade name. The trade name certificate does not give you any legal right to use your trade name, and it will not prevent other people from using the exact same trade name for the exact same type of business in the same town or city. All the certificate does is serve as a public notice that if anyone gets hit by a truck with "Cliff: The Legal Guy" stenciled on the side, the individual named in the certificate is the one who should be sued. The function of a trade name certificate is to prevent people from doing illegal things under the cover of a phony or fictitious name, not to grant exclusive rights to the use of a name.

If you have filed a trade name certificate in your town or city for your home-based business, you have complied with the law. What you have not done is protected your business name.

Registering as an LLC or Corporation

If you decide to incorporate your business by forming a corporation or limited liability company (LLC), you will be required to file a piece of paper (called a "Certificate of Incorporation" for a corporation and "Articles of Organization" for an LLC) with the Secretary of State's office of the state in which your business will operate. On this piece of paper you will be required to designate your business name, followed by the letters "INC." or "CORP." for a corporation and "L.L.C." for an LLC. If someone else has filed a Certificate of Incorporation or Articles of Organization for a company having the exact same name, your piece of paper will not be filed. It will be rejected and returned to you with a request that you

select another name. Similarly, if your piece of paper is filed and someone else wants to form a corporation or LLC using exactly the same name, their piece of paper will be rejected. The first person to file with the Secretary of State's office gets the exclusive right to use that name when doing business within the state.

It sounds straightforward enough, right? Many people think that by forming a corporation or LLC and registering their name with the Secretary of State's office that they have done all they need to do to protect their business name legally.

Sadly, that is not the case. The protection you get by filing incorporation papers is only a very limited protection. Here are two of the limitations.

First, registering your corporate or LLC name with the Secretary of State's office gives you protection only for business done within the state. If you do business in another state and another business has previously registered its name with the Secretary of State's office in that state, the other company will not allow you to use the same name in that state. So if I form "Cliff: The Legal Guy L.L.C." in Connecticut and open an office in New York, where there is already a "Cliff: The Legal Guy Corporation" registered in Albany, the New York company can write me a nasty letter insisting that I cease and desist using that name when doing business in New York. Similarly, I can write the New York company a nasty letter, if I find they want to open an office in Connecticut.

For example, if this should ever happen to your business, register your business name with "of [Name of State]" tacked on at the end. So, in the preceding example, when I receive the nasty letter from the New York company, I can register the name "Cliff: The Legal Guy of New York, L.L.C." with the Secretary of State's office in Albany. Because my name is not exactly the same as the New York company's (because of the "of New York" I've tacked on at the end), the Secretary of State's office will allow me to register my name, and I will be home free. Well, not quite, as we will see later.

Second, if someone with an unincorporated business (such as a sole proprietorship or partnership) is using the name "Cliff: The Legal Guy" and I just don't know about it, registering my corporation or LLC name with the Secretary of State's office will not prevent me from getting sued by the unincorporated business for ripping off their name. An unincorporated business, by definition, is not required to register its name with any state government agency. But that does not prevent them from having the legal right to use that name or from suing others who try to capitalize on that name without permission. Similarly, if I register a corporation or LLC name with the Secretary of State's office and someone else decides it's a cool name and starts an unincorporated business with the same name, the fact that I've registered the name with the state does not mean that I technically "own" it and will be able to prevent the usurper from using it.

Registering a Trademark or Copyright

The only way to protect a business name legally is to seek protection under the federal or state trademark laws (discussed in this section) or the federal copyright laws (discussed in the next section).

When we talk about trademarks and copyrights, what are we really talking about? Most people think, when they obtain a trademark or a copyright on something, that they "own" that something in a way that no one can ever take away from them. Actually, that's not the case. A trademark or copyright is a "legal monopoly"—the right to exclude others for a certain period of time from using the same trademark or copyrighted

words without your permission. Because trademarks and copyrights are exceptions to the government's overall policy against monopolies (as embodied in the antitrust laws and elsewhere), trademarks and copyrights are governed by rather strict legal rules. If you fail to comply with these rules, you lose your legal monopoly.

What is a "trademark" (in the case of goods and products) or "service mark" (in the case of services)? It is literally a "mark" that you put on your goods and products or on the hardware you use in providing services (such as your truck, stationery, and business cards) to identify where they come from. Your business name may or may not be a trademark or service mark, depending on whether or not you actually use it in commerce. For example, let's say you start a home-based publishing business and call it "XYZ Corporation." When you buy a Xerox copying machine, you know it was manufactured by Xerox Corporation. But does the copier have "Xerox Corporation" printed on the side? Probably not. The machine probably just says "Xerox," followed by the model number. In this case, "Xerox Corporation" is not a trademark because it is not actually being used on the company's products, but "Xerox" is a trademark. Get the picture? In order to qualify your business name as a trademark, you must actually put it (without modification) on your products or on the hardware you use to provide services. When you file for a federal trademark for a particular name, the U.S. Patent and Trademark Office in Washington, D.C., will require proof that you are actually using that name, verbatim, in commerce.

There are two types of trademark: common law trademarks and registered trademarks. Common law trademarks are indicated by the letters "TM" (in the case of goods and services) and "SM" (in the case of services) in the upper right-hand corner of the mark. To claim a common law trademark you do not have to file any piece of paper with any government agency. The "TM" or "SM" merely stands as notice to the world that "I'm using these words, symbols, or logo as trademarks, and if you try to steal them by putting them or something very similar on your products and services, I'm going to sue you." You can claim a common law trademark on just about anything, but beware—common law trademarks are very weak. If someone else using a similar mark can prove he or she was using it in commerce before you were, not only can't you stop them from using their mark, but also they can come after you and make you cease and desist using your mark!

Registered trademarks are indicated by the letter "R" in a circle and can only be granted by the U.S. Patent and Trademark Office in Washington, D.C. **It is a Federal crime to use the letter "R" in a circle if you haven't registered your mark with the U.S. Patent and Trademark Office.** Registered trademarks are not easy to come by; they will cost approximately $500 to $750 in legal and filing fees, plus the cost of a "search" (which I highly recommend) to determine that your mark is not confusingly similar to someone else's already registered mark. The total cost of registering a trademark is likely to be between $1,000 and $2,000 (more if you use a large law firm in a major city). The U.S. Patent and Trademark Office is currently clogged with thousands of applications, so it may take several months from the time your application is filed to the time the registered trademark is granted.

Your business name may or may not qualify for registration with the U.S. Patent and Trademark Office. Not only must you actually use it in commerce (the U.S. Patent and Trademark Office will want proof of that), but also the mark must be "distinctive" in some way—something that has an element of originality in it. For example, if you come up with a new type of child-friendly putty and decide to call it "Gooble-dygopp," you will probably be able to register "Goobledygopp" as a trademark. Why? If you go to your local library and look

up "Goobledygopp" in the *Oxford English Dictionary*, you will not see a listing for "Goobledygopp." Words that are used in the English language or are listed in the *Oxford English Dictionary* most likely cannot be trademarked, even if you arrange them in a distinctive way. For example, "Cliff's LLC Service" probably will not be trademarkable because all three of these words exist in common usage (there are other people named Cliff, after all). You cannot claim a legal monopoly on words or combinations of words that already exist in the English language (or indeed in any other language—"Los Servicios LLC de Cliff" probably would not be able to be registered as a trademark either).

So what are your options if your name consists of commonly used English words? Basically, you have two options. First, you can claim your business name as a common law trademark by adding "TM" or "SM" after the name and keep your fingers crossed that there isn't anyone else out there using the same or a confusingly similar name. Second, you can hire a graphic designer to create an original "logo" that incorporates your business name as an integral element. For example, the name "Burger King" by itself probably is not trademarkable ("Burger" and "King" are both commonly used words), but the Burger King logo—a stylized hamburger with the words "Burger King" where the meat is supposed to go—certainly is a registered trademark.

There is a third option for small service-type businesses that operate only within a limited area of a particular state. Most states have trademark laws that allow you to register a trademark for use in that state only. As very few businesses apply for state trademarks, the government offices are usually not that busy and will be more flexible in granting registration for your mark. The downside is that a state trademark is only valid within that state; if you are doing any interstate commerce at all, the trademark will not help you when you do business in other states. Moreover, if someone in another state is using the same mark and has registered it with the U.S. Patent and Trademark Office, they can force you to cease and desist using your mark even if the other company is not technically doing business in your state. Finally, the cost of registering a state trademark or service mark is about the same as registering with the U.S. Patent and Trademark Office. I usually advise clients that it's a waste of their time and money to pursue a state-registered trademark or service mark when they can get better protection at the federal level (a federally registered mark protects you in all fifty states) at about the same cost.

The last thing you need to know about trademarks and service marks is that "if you don't use them, you lose them." You must actually use the mark in commerce; if you cease to use the mark, sooner or later you lose your monopoly, and others can benefit from the use of your mark. More importantly, if you discover that someone else in the United States is using a confusingly similar mark to your own for a similar product or service, you must notify them of the similarity and do everything you can to make them stop using the similar mark. You must be vigorous in protecting your mark against infringers. For example, when you blow your nose into a soft tissue, what do you call the tissue? If you are like most folks, you call it a "Kleenex." Once upon a time, "Kleenex" was the registered trademark of a large Fortune 500 company that invented the concept of the soft facial tissue. Because this company did not vigorously protect its mark, the word became part of common usage and therefore could no longer be trademarked.

The Federal Copyright Laws

An original literary work or other arrangement of words can be copyrighted. Like trademarks and service marks, there are two types of copyrights. A common law copyright is obtained by putting the federal copyright notice next to it—the letter "C" in a circle or the word "copyright," followed by the year of first publication, followed by the name of the person claiming the copyright, followed by "all rights reserved," for example, "© 1999 Clifford R. Ennico. All Rights Reserved". Clearly this is not practical for a business name, which will usually consist only of one to three words.

Technically, there is no reason why a business name or slogan cannot be copyrighted. Filing a copyright application is relatively simple, and it grants basically the same protection as a federally registered trademark.

"Tickets to a Courtroom"

Keep in mind, however, that trademarks and copyrights are nothing more than "tickets to a courtroom," and they do not enforce themselves. While registering your business name as a trademark, service mark, or copyright will grant you some protection against people using confusingly similar names, you will still be required to bring a lawsuit and spend thousands of dollars and months of your life enforcing the trademark, service mark, or copyright. If your business is purely local in nature, is not intended to become a consumer "brand," and doesn't have a distinctive name, the cost of obtaining a federally registered trademark, service mark, or copyright is probably not justified by the benefit you will receive.

One Last Point about Names

Don't be too cute when naming your company. Even though your name will not technically infringe on another company's registered trademark or copyright, it can get you into a lot of trouble.

If you have invented a super-thin, super-light bathroom tissue and are thinking about calling it "Micro-Soft Tissue," at least one company (although in an unrelated industry) may want to have a few words with you. Their argument will be that your name "disparages" the computer software giant in the marketplace, and are they really wrong?

CHAPTER 4

CROOKS, FLAKES, AND FRAUDS— IN A WORD, "THIEVES"

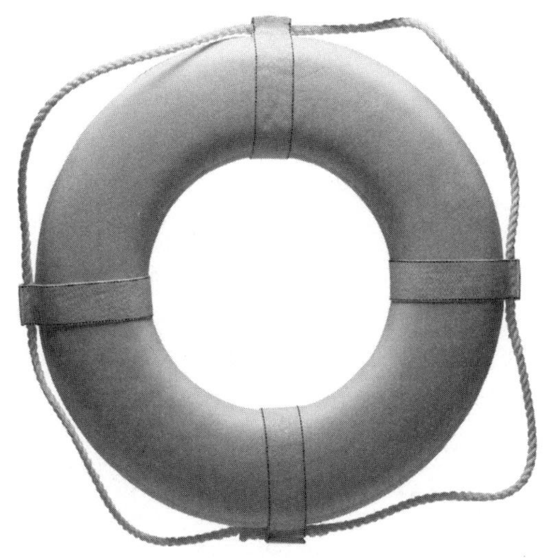

This chapter deals with crooks and thieves of all sorts, both people and inanimate objects, which try to rob your business of its most precious assets—money, property, ideas, and your most valuable asset of all, time.

Preventing Theft of Tangible Goods

Businesses, like residences, are subject to burglary and theft. Shame on you if you don't have some basic security systems in place, such as:

- Locks on the doors (please don't laugh; you don't know some of my clients).
- Bars on the windows, if you are in a high-crime area
- Alarm systems.
- A heavy safe, bolted to the floor, preferably in a place (such as an attic or basement, or even—no kidding—an outhouse) where burglars don't look for valuables.
- A vicious, barking dog. Rottweilers are good for this; Pomeranians won't cut it, no matter how aggressive.
- Removing any foliage, trees, or signage close to your business premises that would enable burglars to gain entry without being overlooked by neighbors or police patrols.

If you are in a high-crime area because it's important for you to keep your real estate costs as low as possible, consider moving to a rural area, where real estate costs are also low but there's less likelihood of violent crime. You may be able to get incentives from some local business development agencies, which will be absolutely thrilled that you want to move into town and create some much-needed jobs.

Preventing the Theft of Ideas and Trade Secrets

In recent years, as careers have become more "mobile" and as employee loyalty has declined, companies have taken more aggressive steps to protect their businesses against "unfair" competition from former employees. The key word is "unfair." It is against public policy in virtually every state to deny an individual the right to earn a living merely because his employment by a particular employer has been terminated. However, a small business should be able to protect itself from having its skilled employees "jump ship" to a local competitor. Such protection can be accomplished by four agreements:

1. A "confidentiality" agreement, by which the employee agrees to keep the employer's confidential information proprietary.
2. An "agreement not to solicit," by which the employee agrees not to solicit customers or employees for a fixed period of time after the termination of his or her employment.
3. An "agreement not to compete," by which the employee agrees not to work for a competitor within a fixed period of time after the termination of his or her employment.
4. An "ownership of intellectual property" agreement, by which the employee agrees that any inventions, ideas, concepts, etc., developed by the employee in the course of employment belongs exclusively to the employer.

A simple, "plain English" Noncompete Agreement for a service or clerical employee appears as **Form 1** (see page 222). For a sample "Assignment of Rights" clause for a consultant or independent contractor, visit www.cliffennico.com.

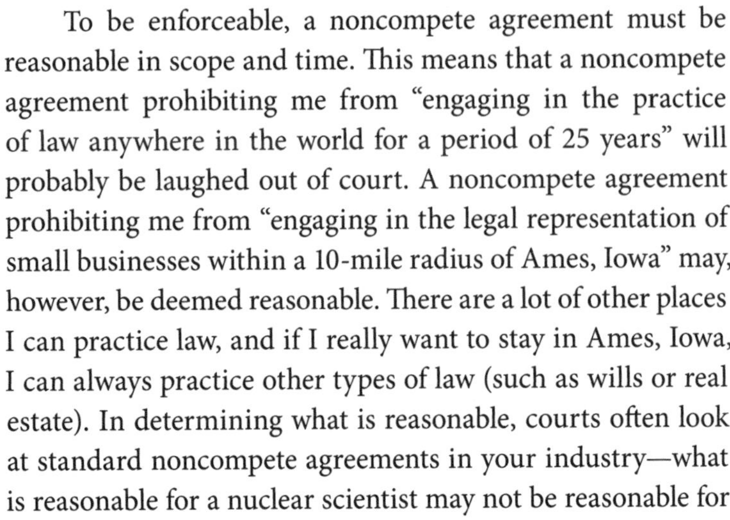

To be enforceable, a noncompete agreement must be reasonable in scope and time. This means that a noncompete agreement prohibiting me from "engaging in the practice of law anywhere in the world for a period of 25 years" will probably be laughed out of court. A noncompete agreement prohibiting me from "engaging in the legal representation of small businesses within a 10-mile radius of Ames, Iowa" may, however, be deemed reasonable. There are a lot of other places I can practice law, and if I really want to stay in Ames, Iowa, I can always practice other types of law (such as wills or real estate). In determining what is reasonable, courts often look at standard noncompete agreements in your industry—what is reasonable for a nuclear scientist may not be reasonable for a hair stylist.

These agreements are not "ironclad," and there is no guarantee they will be enforceable in all situations. For example, in California a noncompete agreement that extends beyond the expiration or termination of the employment relationship is not enforceable except in certain limited situations. Here it is important for the business owner to consider when to ask its employees to sign such agreements. Generally, agreements of this nature are more likely to be enforceable if they are signed as a condition to employment or if additional consideration, such as a "sign-on" bonus, is offered for the agreement. However, agreements required as a condition of continued employment are less likely to be enforceable and can create obvious employee relations issues.

Dealing with Fraud

We all think we know what fraud is, but what is it anyway?

Fraud, broadly defined, is a "knowing misstatement of a material fact." That's a mouthful, but here's what it boils down to:

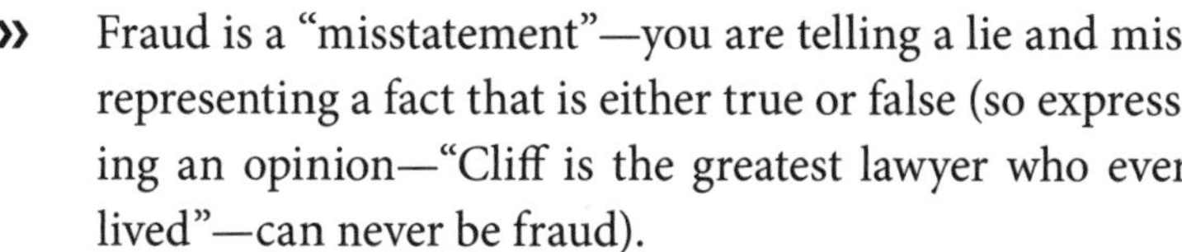

- Fraud is a "misstatement"—you are telling a lie and misrepresenting a fact that is either true or false (so expressing an opinion—"Cliff is the greatest lawyer who ever lived"—can never be fraud).
- Fraud can be overt (you make a false statement—"I am the owner of legal title to the Brooklyn Bridge") or covert (you make a statement that is true as far as it goes but leave out other information that, if known, would make your statement false). If, for example, you say an antique is in "100 percent original working order" when you know the item has been completely repainted within the last year by a kindergarten student, you are committing fraud if your buyer relies on your statement.
- You have to know you're lying—if you believe in good faith something is true but it isn't, you're not committing fraud (though your customers will think you are incompetent).
- The fact must be "material" (i.e., something we would rely on in making a business decision). If you say your gross sales last year were $1 million when they really were $990,000, that's probably not material, but if your actual sales were $800,000, your $1 million sales quote would probably be a material misstatement of fact.

Checking Out Potential Partners, Employees, and Consultants

Here are some things to consider if you are thinking of creating a partnership or hiring an employee or consultant.

Reference Checks

When someone approaches you as a potential partner, employee, or independent contractor, you should check them

out. It's estimated that about one-third of job applicants lie about their experiences and educational achievements on their resumes or job applications.

But merely calling former employers or clients for "reference checks" may not be enough because of the fear of lawsuits. Fearful of reprisals from former employees or consultants, many companies will not give detailed reference information. The Human Resources Department is likely to limit their answer to "dates of employment, job title, and salary."

For best results, try to circumvent the Human Resources Department and go directly to the candidate's former supervisor or the person who was the "direct contact" with an independent consultant. Sometimes they're in a chatty mood and aren't aware of the legal restrictions their companies impose on conversations regarding former employees or consultants.

If the supervisor says "I only give good references" and doesn't elaborate or damns the candidate with faint praise, take the hint. You've got your answer.

"Googling" Candidates on the Internet

You can search the Internet using the candidate's name, look him or her up at university and former employer sites, and cruise news archives for postings to chat groups and "blogs" (short for Weblog, sort of an online diary).

The problem, of course, is that the information you will see online may not be reliable or even relevant to the position for which the candidate is being considered. What if you see a "blog" from the candidate's former romantic partner describing in exquisite detail the candidate's . . . uh . . . preferences? Should that influence your hiring decision?

If you use the Web to check out job applicants, always confirm the information with the candidate in a follow-up interview or phone call and don't let your final decision hinge on what you find out over the Internet.

Oh, and another thing . . . be prepared for questions from the candidate about your own background. Internet searches are a two-way street, after all.

Hiring Private Investigators

Private investigators (PIs) don't just skulk around in parked cars spying on cheating spouses anymore. A lot of their work centers on using the Internet and other software products to conduct wide-ranging searches about people's backgrounds. And no . . . they don't still wear trench coats and sunglasses.

A private investigator can access records you would have a tough time getting access to and can come up with an amazing amount of detailed information about a person, although it will cost you. Depending on your part of the country, a PI's rates can range from $50 to $200 an hour, although you might be able to control the fee by limiting the amount of time you want him or her to spend on a particular search.

Where do you find PIs? Try the telephone book. Just about every state has an association of private investigators that will give you a list of its members in your community. For a listing of these organizations, type "association of private investigators" into your preferred search engine.

What should you look for in a PI?

- Make sure they have a license—almost all states require PIs to be licensed and bonded.
- Always get a written contract—spell out why you are hiring the PI and what results you want to obtain.
- Check out their experience—do they have a background in investigation and surveillance, or are they merely military or law enforcement retirees who do PI work to get out of the house every once in a while?

» Make sure they're insured—PIs get into automobile accidents just like everyone else, and your insurance should not be covering their errors and omissions.

Be careful. There are many companies offering services on the Internet that do not qualify as "investigations." Most of these companies are "information brokers" who have access to records—such as telephone numbers, address directories, and "background checks"—that are simply public record searches. With a little training, you can do most of these types of searches yourself. Remember you get what you pay for.

Time Vampires

Which is more important, money or time? It sounds like a silly question, since you can't really pay for a candy bar by giving the vendor "five minutes." But I humbly submit that, when you run your own business, time is more valuable than money. If you make a bad business deal or squander some money on some useless "antiques" that turn out to be bogus reproductions, you can always make it back on the next deal or work a little harder and generate a few more hourly fees from clients.

When you devote a significant amount of time to something, however, and it ends up going nowhere, you will never get that time back. It's gone forever. Maybe you learned something from the experience. Education is always worth something, but you can't make it back no matter how hard you work or how smart you are. We only have so much time in life, and making the most use of every precious minute is Priority Number One.

That's why I'm so impatient with people and things that try to waste my time. The office colleague who stops by your office two or three times a day looking for free advice for his clients, the former student who e-mails you daily with legal questions he doesn't want to pay for, and the entrepreneur who wants you to set up a franchise for his hot new retail concept and promises he will "pay you as soon as the first franchised outlet opens" are all what I call Time Vampires. They wouldn't like it if you said it to their faces, but they are as much "thieves" as any professional burglar.

The toughest part of dealing with Time Vampires is that they're such nice people usually. They don't understand that they are taking up your valuable time, and they don't see themselves as encroaching on your success. They see themselves, if anything, as friends, and you are a "buddy" who can be trusted with their innermost confidences.

We all need friends, and I'm not suggesting that you only interact with people who bring you business or help you make money. Sometimes the best thing you can do to get your mind off the stress and pressure of running a business is meet an old buddy at a local watering hole, have a couple of beers, and waste a couple of hours talking about your lives and reminiscing about the old days. If you make a regular habit of it, however, you risk wasting too much time and giving away too many products or services to people who don't deserve it and should just "get a life."

CHAPTER 5

SUPPLIERS, CUSTOMERS, EMPLOYEES, AND CONTRACTORS: KEEPING THEM HAPPY

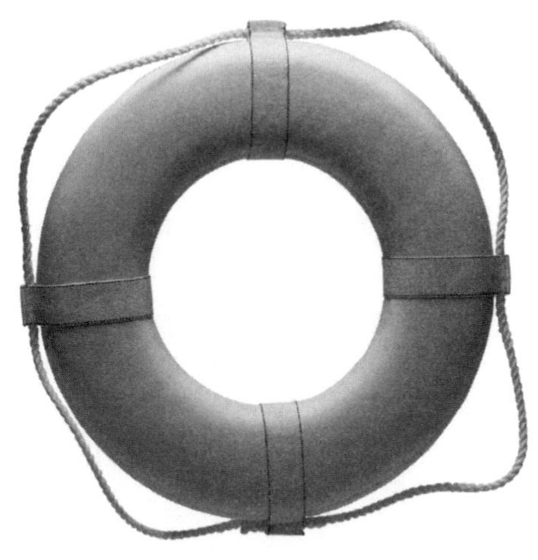

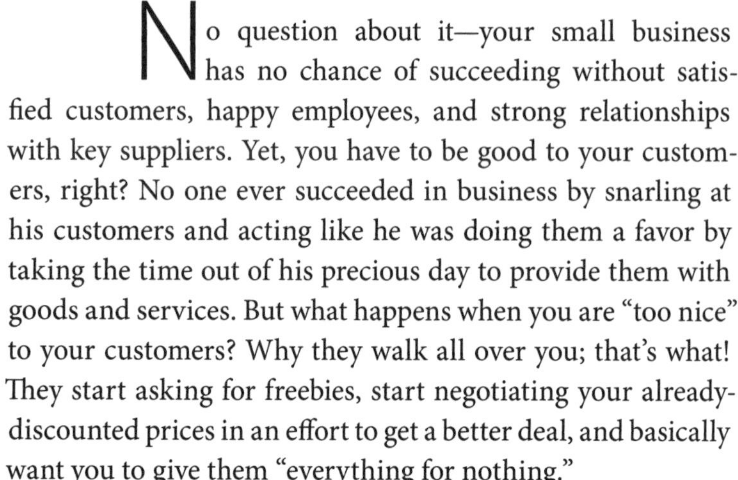

No question about it—your small business has no chance of succeeding without satisfied customers, happy employees, and strong relationships with key suppliers. Yet, you have to be good to your customers, right? No one ever succeeded in business by snarling at his customers and acting like he was doing them a favor by taking the time out of his precious day to provide them with goods and services. But what happens when you are "too nice" to your customers? Why they walk all over you; that's what! They start asking for freebies, start negotiating your already-discounted prices in an effort to get a better deal, and basically want you to give them "everything for nothing."

Now, let's talk about your employees. As a business owner, you want to create a positive, nurturing environment for them, right? After all, you know what it's like to be treated like a galley slave by your previous employers, and you want to do a better job in your own business. Also, you know that these folks could be making better money elsewhere, but they won't leave you, even for a higher salary, if they are happy, contented, and believe that they are being treated fairly. But what happens when you are "too nice" to your employees? They start slacking off on the job, showing up drunk for work (or not at all), and start demanding all kinds of perks and benefits you cannot afford.

Finally, let's talk about your suppliers. You want to develop strong relationships with your key suppliers and encourage them to treat you as a favored customer. But what happens when you're "too nice" to them? Sooner or later, you find that they're selling stuff directly to your customers, or to your archcompetitors, or otherwise trying to circumvent your relationship in favor of a better deal.

This chapter offers some suggestions on keeping your customers, employees, and suppliers motivated, without giving them the keys to your kingdom.

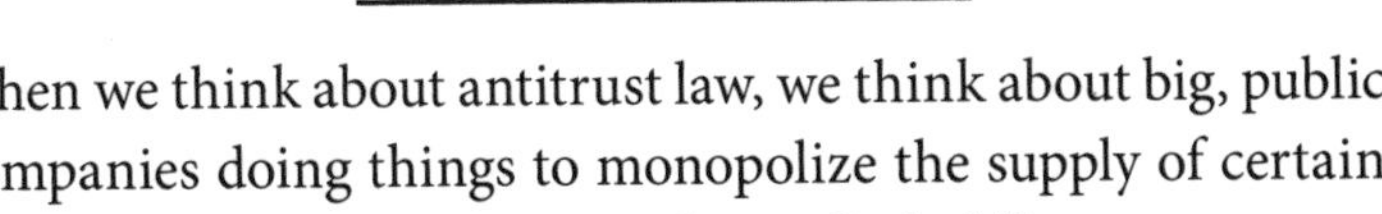

Keeping Your Suppliers at Bay

When we think about antitrust law, we think about big, public companies doing things to monopolize the supply of certain products. We don't think it applies to little folks.

The following e-mail is a classic example of why even the smallest business needs to be concerned about agreements that restrict competition in the marketplace:

> *I have a small company that manufactures an electronic component that is used in making video game consoles. I also act as worldwide distributor for another small company—let's call it Acme Corporation—that manufactures a similar component using a different technology.*
>
> *Our relationship with Acme was forged over a year ago. My company provided some advance money to help start up Acme's manufacturing operation and agreed to purchase 5,000 of Acme's components for $50,000. We then began to market Acme's products together with our own and invested an additional $30,000 in marketing costs (such as print advertising in trade journals, a new Web site that featured Acme's products, and contacts with experts in the field). We sold a few Acme products, some directly to customers and some through other distributors, but not nearly enough to recoup our $50,000 investment in Acme, much less the additional $30,000 in marketing costs.*
>
> *We have never had a formal written agreement with Acme. While they never promised us that we would be their exclusive distributor, we have recently learned that Acme has contacted other distributors and that they want to sell their products directly to customers we have introduced to them. Needless to say, we want to do*

something to protect our substantial investment but are not sure how to go about it.

While we are comfortable that Acme can deal with other distributors, we do not want a pricing issue to draw a customer to one of us versus the other. We have proposed that, as between Acme and my company, we would charge the same prices for the same quantities of Acme's products. We also want Acme to agree that they will not sell to any other distributor if the distributor will be reselling at prices lower than those we charge our customers. Do you see any problems with this arrangement?

Oh boy, do I ever!

First, the fact that you and Acme are manufacturing components for the same products, for presumably the same customers, means that you are technically competitors. Any agreement between competitors to fix prices, as you propose, is absolutely illegal under the federal antitrust laws. There's even a possibility you can be thrown in jail if the violation is blatant enough.

Second, your proposed agreement with Acme that they will not sell to another distributor if the distributor resells at a price lower than yours is called "resale price maintenance," another big no-no under the antitrust laws. While a manufacturer may suggest prices at which distributors can resell their goods, it cannot require that distributors resell the products at a fixed markup or put a "floor" under resale prices.

Since you have invested heavily in Acme, you certainly have a right to insist that they help you recoup that investment. In order for any agreement with Acme to work legally, though, it will have to permit Acme to set wholesale and retail prices freely based on Acme's costs, the competition, and market demand. Specifically, you should ask Acme for the following:

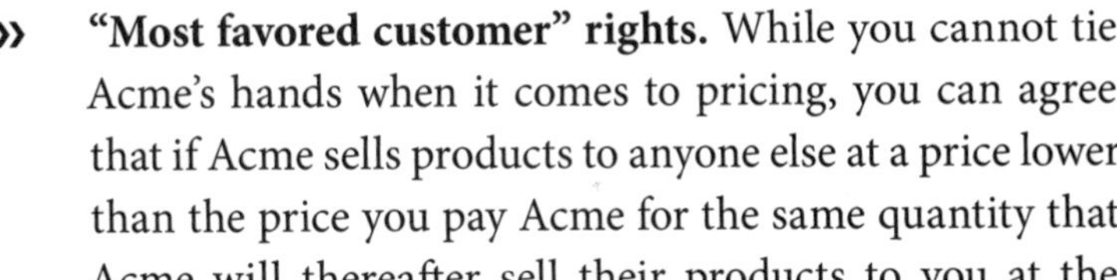

» **"Most favored customer" rights.** While you cannot tie Acme's hands when it comes to pricing, you can agree that if Acme sells products to anyone else at a price lower than the price you pay Acme for the same quantity that Acme will thereafter sell their products to you at the same, lower price; and

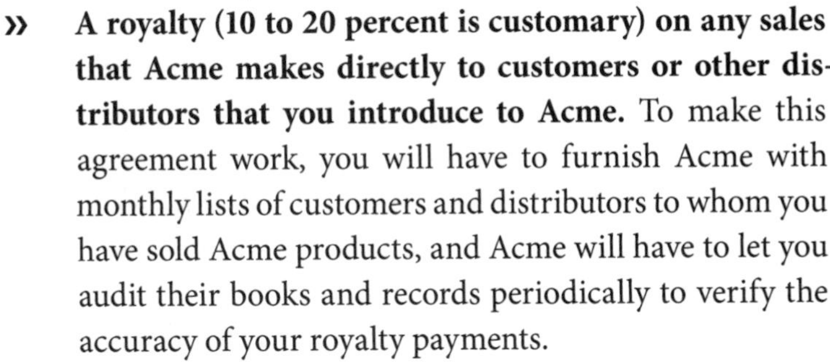

» **A royalty (10 to 20 percent is customary) on any sales that Acme makes directly to customers or other distributors that you introduce to Acme.** To make this agreement work, you will have to furnish Acme with monthly lists of customers and distributors to whom you have sold Acme products, and Acme will have to let you audit their books and records periodically to verify the accuracy of your royalty payments.

Both of these agreements are perfectly legal and will help you recoup your investment and become a "key" distributor, if not the only one, of Acme's products.

If it were my money, I would also get Acme to agree (1) that your $80,000 investment in Acme is a loan, secured by a mortgage on Acme's assets and (2) that if you have not recouped your $80,000 investment within the next twelve months, you will be entitled to convert that "debt" into a significant percentage of Acme stock (at least 20 percent). The prospect of having an angry distributor as a major stockholder should put some much-needed pressure on Acme's executives to steer business your way.

Motivating Your Employees Without Giving Away the Store

It's one of the classic "Goldilocks" problems in running any business.

If you push your employees too hard to get results, they resent you. They talk about you behind your back and complain bitterly about working in a "sweatshop environment" where their lives are sacrificed to make you rich. The first chance they get, they bolt to another company, probably a competitor. Read any installment of the cartoon strip *Dilbert*, and you'll see what I mean.

Yet, if you are too nice to your employees and bend over backward trying to make your workplace as happy, nurturing, and fun-filled as you possibly can, what happens then? Your employees start thinking you are a "soft touch" and start taking advantage of your good nature. They ask for more, more, and more, even though what you're giving them as compensation is quite generous by industry standards. They start showing up drunk for work, or not at all, and play to your sympathies when you try to pull them up short or criticize them. They start second-guessing your management decisions and insist that you justify everything you want or need them to do.

How can you get your employee relationships "just right"? How can you build a positive, healthy working environment for your employees without giving away the store?

Here are some tips on handling employee relations.

You're Not "The Boss"

Today's workers have been taught to "question authority" at all levels and will resent you presenting yourself as an authority figure. You can't just tell people to do something because "you're the boss," because that won't cut it anymore.

The key is to make sure your employees don't see you as "someone who is generous or stingy," but rather someone who is smart and able enough to build a successful company and who will make sure that if the company is prosperous,

the workers who make a difference will become prosperous as well.

But You're Not Their Friend, Either

When you are just getting your business off the ground with only a handful of employees working in close quarters, you inevitably get very close to certain individuals, and that can sometimes be a problem for you, especially if you have to fire them. Once a company has grown beyond the start-up phase, individuals can no longer run the business. You have to put policies in place, put people in charge of managing the policies, and let all employees know that their success will depend upon their adherence to the policies, not their personal relationship with you.

Make the Company the "Third Person in the Room"

Employees should be thinking of the company's well-being, not yours. You should make a point of telling employees that thus-and-such goal will benefit the company as a whole and therefore benefit everyone. By putting the company in the room along with you and the employee and telling the employee if that artificial third person is happy that they will be happy as well, they will see the alignment between the company's best interests and their own.

Make Incentives on a Group Basis, Not an Individual Basis

Bonuses and other incentives should be based upon the company's performance, not solely on the individual employee's performance. Consider establishing a productivity bonus, where you set output goals for a particular operation or function, and make sure people know that if, for example, the whole plant

produces more product per employee-hour and meets the quota, then everyone benefits, while if the quantity is surpassed, everyone in that plant gets a bonus for the week. One of the side benefits of this approach is that all employees are guaranteed to be tough on slackers, whiners, and other drags on productivity, knowing that substandard performance will affect them personally.

Be Humane

If your business is located in the Deep South, it gets hot in the summertime, doesn't it? Don't wait for your employees to ask—air-condition your offices and plants. If that's not possible, put fans and water coolers all over the place in your offices and plants, as well as "blow fans" with evaporated water that fees like air-conditioning.

Make Your Employees "See the Logic"

While you shouldn't have to explain yourself constantly to your employees, it's important to make employees see the logic in what you're doing. If people can see why what you're doing makes sense, if they can see the logic of what you're doing, and that it does make business sense and does create value, they will not view it as an arbitrary "order from the boss" that has to be challenged.

As Benjamin Franklin said back in 1776, as British forces approached the fledgling colonial capital of Philadelphia, "We must all hang together, or assuredly we shall all hang separately."

The Employment Agreement

Should you have an agreement with your employees? Well, it depends. For low-level clerical and manufacturing employees,

it probably isn't a good idea, since they're not accustomed to signing legal contracts. They may not understand the contract well, and they are unlikely to hire a lawyer to interpret it.

For anyone having access to your business's sensitive information, a short, well-drafted employment agreement is a must. Often, the letter offering employment to a "new hire" will contain many of the important provisions required in an employment agreement. See **Form 4** (page 234) for a sample "employment offer" letter containing the most important legal requirements.

Preventing Lawsuits from Ex-Employees

Firing an employee, especially one you've worked with for awhile, is probably one of the hardest things you will ever do when running a business. Yet, if you don't do it, you send a strong signal to all of your employees that bad behavior or sloppy performance will be overlooked. Employers who send those signals soon lose control of their operations, and failure is almost a certainty.

You know it's time to fire an employee when one or more of the following things are true:

- They are not performing up to your expectations.
- They are violating the law.
- They are dragging down your performance or the morale of other employees. ("If Cliff can get away with thus-and-such, why should I be killing myself?")
- You simply cannot afford to keep them.

Yet, if you aren't careful about how you handle the firing, you may be opening the door to a "wrongful termination" lawsuit from a disgruntled ex-employee who feels you were unfair or arbitrary in your decision to terminate them. There are three

steps to avoiding such lawsuits: make sure there are no surprises; conduct a proper exit interview; and follow up the termination promptly so as not to disrupt your operations.

"No Surprises"

If a firing comes as a surprise to an employee, you are much more likely to be sued for wrongful termination. Make sure you carefully document the employee's performance, give them at least one "fair warning" and a chance to turn things around, with a specific deadline for them to meet. If the deadline is not met, give them an ultimatum to achieve certain specific results by a certain date "or else" (a colleague of mine calls these "fee-fi-fo-fum" meetings).

Be flexible because circumstances can surprise you. I once had a client who ran a small retail store with only one employee—a part-time female clerk. The clerk persistently showed up late, spent most of her time at work making personal calls on her cell phone, and refused to do any work that involved physical or manual labor. My client was fed up and, on my advice, gave the clerk a warning that if her attitude and behavior did not improve (she gave very specific examples of goals the employee was to meet) by a certain date, she would be terminated. The employee's performance did not improve. On the morning of the termination date, the employee walked into the store (late, as usual) and, before my client could say anything, announced to the entire store "Hey, everybody, congratulate me—I just found out I'm pregnant!"

Fortunately, my client had the foresight not to proceed with the firing and called me immediately. Had she fired the employee, she almost certainly would have been hit with a lawsuit from the employee, who would have claimed that her pregnancy and not her performance was the cause of termination. We adopted a different strategy for that employee, which

fortunately was never needed, since the employee voluntarily quit a couple of weeks later.

The Exit Interview

Here are some tips for conducting a successful exit interview:

- Have a witness present—you never know what disgruntled employees will say or do.
- Explain the performance you expected and the steps you took to help the employee meet his or her performance goals and state clearly and unequivocally that the employee has not met the expectation.
- Do not be vague or emotional, and don't give in if the employee becomes emotional or angry—have a box of Kleenex ready.
- Keep the meeting short and to the point—the less you say, the better it will be.
- Schedule the meeting on a Monday, not a Friday—otherwise the employee will have a chance to "stew" over the weekend.
- Lock the employee out of the computer system before the exit interview, so that the employee doesn't change passwords, delete important data, or otherwise trash their computer. If the employee has access to a laptop computer, make them hand it over at the interview.
- Ask for their keys to the office and the company car and any other company property in their possession.
- Tell the employee what you will say if anyone asks for a reference (this should be cleared with your attorney before the meeting), and tell them you will not challenge their application for unemployment benefits if he or she is eligible for them.

- If you are worried about personal safety, have a building security guard present to escort the employee out of the building.

Following Up the Firing

After the exit interview has been completed and the employee has departed your premises, there are a number of "postfiring" details you have to attend to:

- When the ex-employee applies for unemployment benefits, you will be invited to a hearing to offer any objections to the information the ex-employee has provided on his application for benefits. Unless your attorney advises you otherwise, do not attend the hearing, since anything you say about the ex-employee during the hearing can be used against you in a wrongful termination action, and in most states the ex-employee will receive benefits anyway no matter what you say.
- You should explain the firing to other employees to avoid nasty rumors from spreading. If necessary, you should reassign the ex-employee's duties to other employees as soon as possible, so that there is no disruption of operations and the remaining employees can return to a regular routine quickly. The longer they are looking at a vacant office and an empty box on the organization chart, the more likely you will have to deal with negative office politics as they jockey for position.

"Good Contracts Make Good Clients"

When you are in a service business, what you are really selling your customers is your time. The problem with time, as Will

Rogers once pointed out in a different context (he was talking about real estate), is that "they're not making any more of the stuff." Once you have spent time working on a project, nobody can give you back the lost time. This is why people in service businesses charge money for their services—because the time spent working for one client is time you cannot spend working for another client.

Despite your best efforts, clients often want to play games with your precious time. Do any of these horror stories sound familiar?

- You quote a flat fee for a particular job, based on your best assumption of the number of hours it will take to get the job done. After beginning the job, the client requests additional services and claims that they were part of the flat fee you quoted. When you object (nicely) that the requested services go beyond the original scope of the project, the client accuses you of "changing the deal" and threatens to terminate your contract unless you agree to the additional services.
- You quote a daily rate for a job, based on your assumption that a day consists of eight hours. When you find yourself working 12-hour days on the project and request overtime, you are told that the client expects all service providers to work 12-hour days, "the same as our employees do."
- You quote an hourly rate for a job and agree to submit monthly invoices to the client. You are told that the customer normally pays invoices within 45 days. When your first invoice is not paid within 45 days, you are told that due to a change in the customer's policy all payments are now made within sixty days. When sixty days have passed, you are told that the policy has changed yet again and that payments are now made within ninety days.

When you are a "little person" running a business, you should begin every client relationship with the notion that the client will try to cheat you if they can. As my grandmother used to say, "Assume the worst of everyone you do business with. That way the only surprises you get will be pleasant ones." This is good advice, especially in a difficult economy where even honest, ethical clients are having trouble making ends meet.

To prevent clients from cheating you, you need two things: (1) a written contract that states clearly and precisely what you will do, how you will be paid, and when you will be paid and (2) a working relationship that gives you "leverage" over the client to ensure that if the client's business heads south, you will be one of the lucky few who get paid.

A Good, Solid Contract

You should never, ever perform services for a client on a handshake basis. Every job, even a small one, should have a written agreement. This does not have to be a formal document of ten pages or more written in "legalese." It can be a simple one- or two-page letter, signed by you and countersigned by the client as a "memorandum" of how you will work together. Any good attorney can prepare a standard form for you and should charge only one or two hours of their time.

What should this agreement contain? At the very least:

The services you will perform

The agreement should state clearly what you will do and the tangible results (or "deliverables") the client can expect to receive before you are finished. You should put together a series of "bullets" describing each task and deliverable, type "Exhibit A" at the top of the list, attach the list to the agreement, and state clearly that you will perform "the services described on Exhibit A attached to this letter."

The services you will not perform

The agreement should state clearly what you will not do as part of the project. For example, my retainer letter clearly states that I do not perform litigation services (representing clients in court) under any circumstances. If that is not possible, your agreement should state that "any services requested by Client that are not listed on Exhibit A are not a part of this agreement." That should deter the client who wants to expand the scope of the project without paying any more for the additional work, a process known as "job creep."

The amount you will be paid and the assumptions, if any, underlying your fee quote

If you are quoting a flat fee but want to be reimbursed for out-of-pocket expenses on top of that, be sure to say that the flat fee doesn't include expenses. Otherwise the client will assume that it does. If you are quoting a fee based on a time estimate, say clearly that the quote is "based on an estimate of X days of Y hours each," with the additional statement that "any additional time required by Client will be billed at X dollars per hour." If your calculation of the number of days includes travel time, say so. If the fee quote is based on other assumptions (for example, the number of on-site visits you will have to make or the number of the client's employees you will have to train), spell them out and reserve the right to renegotiate if things turn out to be different.

The key here is to leave the client as little "wiggle room" as possible, so that if and when things change, you are in control of the discussion.

When you will be paid

It is amazing to me how many service professionals—intelligent, highly educated people—forget to put the timetable for payment in their contracts. If the client has promised to pay

your bills within thirty days, put it in the contract. If the client has promised a partial payment at the beginning of the job, put it in the contract. If the client has promised to pay "when the job is finished," describe exactly (use bullet points if necessary) the circumstances under which the job will be considered "finished," so that the client has no "wiggle room."

The consequences to the client if payment is not made

Your agreement must clearly state what you will do (or not do) in the event you do not receive payments on time. Among other things, you should consider the following:

- Charging interest (at "the highest rate allowed by law") on any overdue payment—believe it or not, it is illegal in many states to charge interest on overdue payments without first warning the client you will do so.
- Saying you will stop working on the job, without liability to the client, as long as a scheduled payment is overdue.
- Saying that if payment is not made when due, you will retain all "intellectual property rights" to the work performed for the client, including the right to sell it to other clients (translation: your client's competition).

Obtaining "Leverage" over the Client

Sadly, even a well-drafted contract is often only a "ticket to a courtroom." There are people who will breach contracts with willful abandon if they think they can get away with it.

So, never allow yourself to get into a situation where you do the work first and payment comes later. Always have some sort of "leverage" over the client, so that they have a strong incentive to put you at the top of the payment list when money gets tight, and put it in the contract. Some examples include:

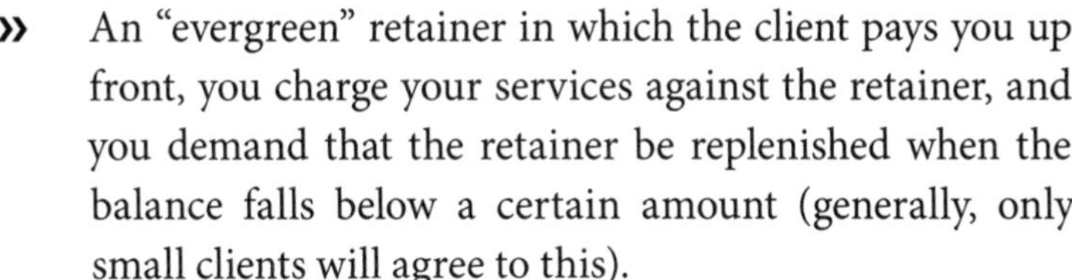

- An "evergreen" retainer in which the client pays you up front, you charge your services against the retainer, and you demand that the retainer be replenished when the balance falls below a certain amount (generally, only small clients will agree to this).
- Scheduling payments at specified stages of the project (called "milestones"), so that the outstanding bill never becomes too large—if payment on Phase I is overdue, you don't begin Phase II until the matter is settled.
- A provision that you will not transfer the rights to your work to the client until final payment has been made (this can be extremely effective, especially for artists, writers, graphic designers, and other "content creators").
- A statement describing other projects the client desperately needs you to do for them—once payment for this job has been fully received.

Managing Your Customers' Expectations: The Subtle Art of "Pest Control"

We are hearing a lot these days about the importance of "multitasking" or, as some human resource experts refer to it, "managing multiple priorities."

The Bible tells us that a person cannot serve many masters, yet for many busy, time-deprived business owners, juggling a number of crises at the same time may be unavoidable.

Imagine what it would be like to be in a business where:

- Every telephone call is a genuine emergency that requires immediate attention.
- You cannot predict the volume of business at any given time.

- Every job is a "little job" for which you cannot charge more than a couple of hundred dollars.
- There is little repeat business from the same customers.
- The costs are such that you cannot have more than one or two employees.

Well, there is such a business—pest control, specifically, the business of removing wild animals from people's homes. If there is a business anywhere in the world where the ability to "multitask" is essential to success, it's this one.

If you have ever had a wild animal (something larger than a mouse) in your home, you know how terrifying it is. Every waking moment is occupied by thoughts of "Where is it?" "Is it eating the food in my pantry?" "Does it have rabies?" "Will I find it crawling into bed with me?" You want your exterminator to sprout wings and fly to you immediately, and each hour's delay in response time is like a dagger in your heart. But what if the exterminator is up to his or her ears in emergency calls?

This is a tale of two pest control firms and how they handled a recent call from someone who woke up one morning to find signs that a large animal had taken up occupancy in the rafters of his basement.

> *Pest Control Firm #1 [the call is answered by the exterminator's answering service]: "We have only one wild animal expert assigned to your town, and he's got a full schedule today. While usually we can squeeze someone into his schedule, we understand he's having some trouble with his equipment and probably will be running behind schedule. We can, however, guarantee that he will be able to stop by your home between 12 noon and 3 P.M. tomorrow. Would you like us to schedule an appointment then?"*

> *Pest Control Firm #2 [the exterminator answers the call from a cell phone in his van]: "Listen, I've got a lot of jobs today, but I'll try to help you if I can. From the way you describe the situation, you've probably got a raccoon down there, so don't disturb him whatever you do. They can turn violent, and the thing might be rabid. Of course, I can't be sure until I get over there. I'm on my way to a job in Town A, then I've got a job in Town B, but you're on my way home, so I'll try to stop by your place sometime between 6 and 10 tonight. I'll call you as soon as I leave my job in Town B." As of 11 P.M. that evening, there was no call from this exterminator, and he never did show up.*

Who did the better job of customer service here? Clearly neither exterminator could do what the customer desperately wanted—send an exterminator over right away—because they were busy handling other emergencies. Firm #1 gave the customer disappointing news, in a rather cold and impersonal manner, but committed to send an exterminator over as soon as his schedule freed up (and lived up to that commitment—the exterminator arrived at 12:05 P.M. the next day).

The second exterminator was more sympathetic and genuinely tried to be helpful by giving the customer some information over the telephone, but succeeded only in scaring the wits out of the customer (needlessly, as it turned out—the intruder turned out to be only a rather chubby mouse), building up the customer's hopes by promising to visit on his way home that evening, and then failing to follow up with either a visit or a telephone call.

It isn't easy to give a customer bad news, especially when there's a genuine emergency. Faced with that situation, the better approach is to be honest and straightforward, tell the customer what you can do, and live up to the commitment

you make. You may still lose some business (the frantic customer will certainly be calling your competitors trying to get a quicker response), but you will at least have preserved their respect. Building up a customer's hopes and then dashing them, even with the best of intentions, is far worse, because now the customer has a negative story to tell about you. And tell it they will.

How to Keep Clients from Becoming Plaintiffs

These days, when customers are dissatisfied, they sue. Three useful tools that can help keep your customers from becoming plaintiffs are legal disclaimers, releases, and "standard terms and conditions of sale." While not 100 percent guaranteed to work in all instances, your chances of successfully fighting a lawsuit are much greater if these are in place than if they aren't.

Disclaimers—A legal disclaimer warns customers that you are not making any warranties about your products or services and that their use of your products and services is "at their own risk." The Web Site Legal Disclaimer available at www.cliffennico.com is a typical disclaimer for a Web site offering products and services.

Releases—If a customer gives you a written release of all claims arising out of a particular activity, they will have a tough time arguing later that you are liable. For a typical General Release of all claims whatsoever arising out of a business relationship, usually signed at the end of the relationship, visit www.cliffennico.com.

Standard Terms and Conditions of Sale—Your invoice forms, purchase orders, and Web sites should contain a document explaining the terms and conditions under which you are willing to sell goods and services to customers generally. While not always enforceable because they are "one-sided" and the customer doesn't generally even know about the terms until after the purchase has been made, "Ts and Cs" give a court at least an opportunity to rule in your favor if the other side is clearly making a bogus claim.

Dealing with Deadbeat Customers and Winning

It happens to the best of us—you sell goods or render a service to a new customer. You send out an invoice and wait thirty, sixty, ninety days. You call and have a friendly conversation with the customer who promises to pay you soon and who requests additional goods and services. You fulfill their request and send out another invoice. Still you receive no payment of the first invoice. Soon you realize that a disproportionate amount of the accounts receivable on your books are from this one customer who is paying slowly, late, or not at all.

Slow-paying and nonpaying customers can kill a small business. While every business should maintain a "reserve for bad debts" on its books for accounting purposes, your goal should be to avoid bad debt situations before they happen and crush "deadbeats" the minute you realize they are posing a threat to your cash flow. No doubt about it, this is an unpleasant task and will call for some ruthlessness on your part, but being nice to people who are threatening your business's success only makes the problem worse.

Here are some effective strategies for dealing with deadbeats.

STRATEGY #1: Choose Your Customers

It's amazing how many times you can spot difficult customers before they even order goods and services from you. If a new customer seems unusually demanding, seems less than candid, is unreasonably vague about details, or refuses to compromise on even minor points of a standard sales contract, be assured that at some point they will become a deadbeat. Trust your instincts. If your nose says "this person's a problem," say no and move on to the next customer.

I realize this is tough advice to follow, especially for new businesses. Often you are happy just to have customers at all and feel compelled to take on whatever business "walks in the door." This can be a fatal mistake, however. Many are the bad people who prey on small, start-up businesses precisely because established, legitimate firms won't do business with them. Don't be afraid to check references and ask about a new client's reputation in the community, and if you don't like what you hear, don't get involved.

In my law practice, for example, I am extremely wary of new clients who complain too much about the services their former lawyer (or former lawyers) performed for them. Now, I'm sure that there are a lot of bad lawyers out there, but there are also a lot of bad clients who make unreasonable demands, ignore sound legal advice, and refuse to pay their bills until their lawyers are compelled to "fire" them. I assume the latter. When a new client starts ranting and raving about his former lawyer, I always ask for the lawyer's name, and then I call him or her for a candid discussion about the client, whether the client permits me to or not (if the client refuses to give me the name, then I terminate the relationship). I think I'm a good enough judge of character to figure out who's telling the truth, and if I'm not sure of the truth after speaking to the client's former lawyer, I don't get involved. The best way to deal with deadbeats is not to get involved with them in the first place.

Also, if you are in a service business, be sure to explain very carefully how much you will charge for your services and how much (and when) you expect to be paid for them. Many deadbeat problems start as simple misunderstandings when naïve clients do not fully realize how much services will cost or when payment is expected. A simple, one-page letter agreement explaining your payment expectations should do the job. Send it by certified mail, return receipt requested, or (better yet) get the client to countersign the letter "accepting and agreeing" to its terms.

STRATEGY #2: Get Paid Up Front

The next best cure for a deadbeat problem is to deal with customers on a "cash on delivery" basis. A friend of mine sells his books and audiotapes through the mail and on the Internet. Frequently he will get orders from distant parts of the country for small amounts of books—sometimes only one or two copies. Unless the order is from an established bookstore chain (such as Barnes & Noble or Borders) that has a centralized order department, my friend always insists on payment in advance. As he puts it, "These people know I'm not about to bring a collection lawsuit in a distant state over a $10 or $20 book—if they want the book that badly, they can pay for it up front."

STRATEGY #3: Charge Interest on Overdue Invoices

Your invoice should state clearly that interest will be charged at the highest rate allowed by law, if payment is not made promptly when due. In most states, you are not allowed to charge interest on overdue debts unless you first warn the customer that this will happen.

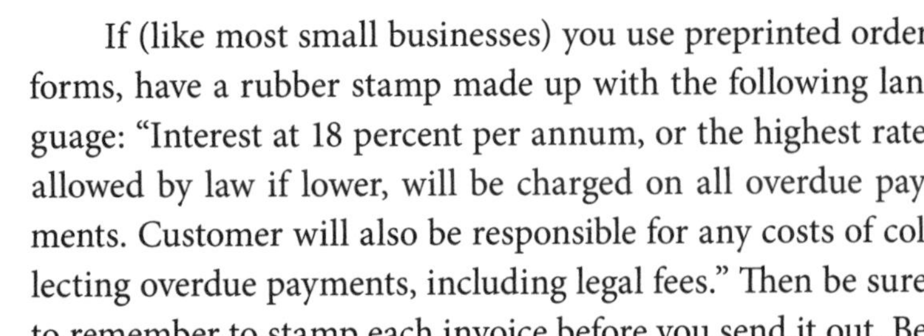

If (like most small businesses) you use preprinted order forms, have a rubber stamp made up with the following language: "Interest at 18 percent per annum, or the highest rate allowed by law if lower, will be charged on all overdue payments. Customer will also be responsible for any costs of collecting overdue payments, including legal fees." Then be sure to remember to stamp each invoice before you send it out. Be sure to use red or purple ink so the customer is sure to see it.

STRATEGY #4: Get Leverage over Your Customer

When a customer becomes a deadbeat, it's very important to have some continuing leverage over the customer. When a business gets into financial trouble, there is usually enough cash on hand to pay some (but not all) of the business's debts. In such a situation, the business will pay only those debts that "absolutely, positively" have to be paid on time—key suppliers, accountants, lawyers, etc. You want to be sure that you are at the top of the food chain so that you get "first call" on that customer's available cash.

As a lawyer, I have very little trouble collecting my debts. People are afraid of lawyers, and they realize that you never want to have a lawyer as an enemy. But people also realize that when they get into legal or financial trouble they need their lawyers more than ever before, and so the lawyers are often the first ones paid. If the customer realizes they will need you to help them get through a difficult period, they will not want you to be unhappy.

Don't be afraid to withhold services, files, or other client property as "security" for your overdue debt. In most states, this is perfectly legal. If a client asks for a "work made for hire" agreement—in which all of your work product automatically becomes the property of the client, add the proviso "provided that I receive all required payments promptly when due." On the rare occasion when a law client slows down payments to me, I gently and politely remind them of some legal matter they will need addressed in the very near future and, in rare cases, will point out that the law allows me to retain all of their client files and sensitive, confidential information as "collateral" for their overdue payments. Believe me, it gets results.

STRATEGY #5: Go Over Their Heads

If your client is a large company, ask for the names of three people in the organization you need to speak to in order to resolve the billing situation, and when you have them, ask for a specific date when you can expect payment before you will be compelled to "go up the chain of command." That will send a strong signal that you are not to be trifled with and that this is a deadline that should be met.

STRATEGY #6: Develop a "Mean" Reputation

I often ask financially distressed clients how they determine who gets paid first and who waits for their payments. Very often, the response is something like, "Well, first, we pay the people who absolutely have to be paid if we are to stay in business. Then we pay the most obnoxious, irritating creditors just to get them off our backs."

If you don't have a lot of leverage over your customers, the only way to get paid may be to become a thorn in their side. Call your deadbeats every day. Bombard them with e-mails. Threaten to contact their customers and other key relationships to report their delinquency. If the amount they owe you is a small one and if they truly believe you are a lunatic, you are highly likely to be paid sooner rather than later. Federal consumer protection law protects individual consumers

against "harassing" collection techniques, but this statute usually does not apply if the deadbeat is a business.

I once had a graphic design client who was owed $1,000 from a customer. When she asked me what to do about it, I told her about small claims court. "No," she responded, "that takes too long. I want to bring a full-blown action in the state courts and put a lien on the guy's house as security for the judgment because I know he's getting ready to refinance his mortgage and can't do it if there's a lien on the house."

I told her it would cost between $2,000 and $3,000 to do all of that and that I didn't think it was worth it to collect a $1,000 debt. She smiled and said, "Sure, that's exactly what my deadbeat wants me to think. I want to send a message to all of my clients that nobody plays around with me. And while you're at it, could you please draft a press release about the suit so I can send it to the local newspapers?" Sure enough, she brought her suit, the customer paid the $1,000 plus her legal fees (which she demanded as a condition to dropping the suit) in record time, and I don't think she has ever had a delinquent customer since.

"Cheat Me Once, Shame on You; Cheat Me Twice, Shame on Me"

It's amazing to me how many small businesses will keep working with customers for long periods of time after they stop making payments on a regular basis. If a customer cheats you once, you can sometimes work it out. But if a customer is becoming a regular and recurring problem, it may be best to drop the customer and cut your losses.

All big accounts receivable start out as small accounts receivable. When a client, especially a large one, starts to drag their feet on payment, it's very tempting to go along for the ride

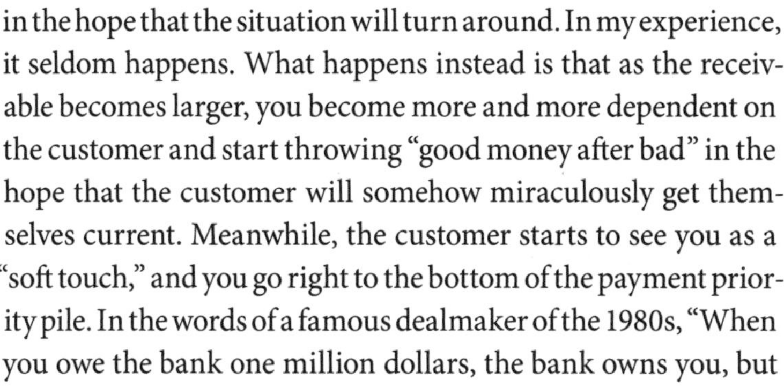

in the hope that the situation will turn around. In my experience, it seldom happens. What happens instead is that as the receivable becomes larger, you become more and more dependent on the customer and start throwing "good money after bad" in the hope that the customer will somehow miraculously get themselves current. Meanwhile, the customer starts to see you as a "soft touch," and you go right to the bottom of the payment priority pile. In the words of a famous dealmaker of the 1980s, "When you owe the bank one million dollars, the bank owns you, but if you owe the bank one BILLION dollars, you own the bank."

The time to nip bad receivables is in the bud. If you cannot get money from a new customer in advance, do a few hours of work, send out a small bill quickly, and see what happens. If the client doesn't respond promptly to the small bill, terminate the relationship. Getting clients in the habit of paying small amounts promptly and often builds solid client relationships later on, when the jobs become bigger, the bills get larger, and you can't afford to write them off.

Bonding with Your Subcontractors

Let's say you are setting up a consulting practice or other service business. You realize that from time to time your clients will need you to perform services you yourself cannot perform. You don't want to hire employees because they're too expensive. You are left with only one alternative: working with subcontractors ("subs" for short) on a job-by-job basis.

Pretty straightforward, right? Well, here are some of the things that can (and often do) go wrong:

» The client doesn't realize the sub is independent of you. The subcontractor makes a mistake, and the client sues you as the sub's "employer."

- Your sub has finished her piece of the job and wants you to pay her "net 30," your client is ninety days past due on your (combined) invoice, and there isn't enough money in your checking account to pay the sub.
- You allow the sub to call and meet with the client directly, and all of a sudden the client is giving new assignments directly to the sub without giving you a shot at the business.

When working with subs, you're sometimes caught between a rock and a hard place. If the sub performs below the client's expectations, it reflects badly on your competence (after all, you picked the sub). If the subcontractor performs above expectations, on the other hand, the client may fall in love with the sub, and you may lose the client relationship. How to navigate this minefield?

A lot of consultants get into trouble by not performing enough "due diligence" on their subs before hiring them. In their eagerness to delegate work, consultants often practice what I call "dump and run": they get assigned a project, dump the work on the subs, and move on to the next project, without really knowing if the sub can do the job or not.

So how do you "kick the tires" when dealing with a new sub? At a minimum, you want to see samples of her work and talk with the sub's previous clients. You should also explain the client's project to the sub in great detail at the outset, to make sure she's following you closely and understands what the client wants.

The key to developing good relationships with subs is to make sure they know that you, not the client, are their customer. This means never allowing your subs to meet with your client unless you yourself are present. Some clients of mine also feel you should pay your subs directly within thirty days and not make them wait until your client pays you. While this may cause some financial pain if a client pays you more slowly than you expected, this may be the price you must pay if you insist that subs treat you, not the client, as the customer.

Here are some other "sub management" techniques that have worked for my clients in the past:

- Guarantee your subs X amount of work a month from you (this will make you more comfortable letting the sub talk directly with your clients).
- Have business cards printed up for the sub with your company logo and a title, such as "of counsel" or "independent representative," that clearly states to clients and others that the sub is not your employee.
- Make sure the sub plans to stay independent for the long run and is not just marking time until the economy improves and she can get a full-time job.

It's important, when dealing with subs, to remember your ultimate goal—making the difficult transition from a "practice" to a "business." In a practice, you're involved in every sales pitch, and then when you sell a client, you do all of the work yourself, whereas in a business, you are managing relationships with clients and overseeing project teams that can interface with the clients. It is impossible to make this transition without developing long-term relationships with subs that can rely on you, not your clients, to provide them with a steady cash flow. Ultimately, that's the best way to keep your subs loyal to you. Nobody wants to kill the goose that's laying golden eggs on a reliable schedule.

CHAPTER 6

THE GOVERNMENT: YOUR BIGGEST PARTNER

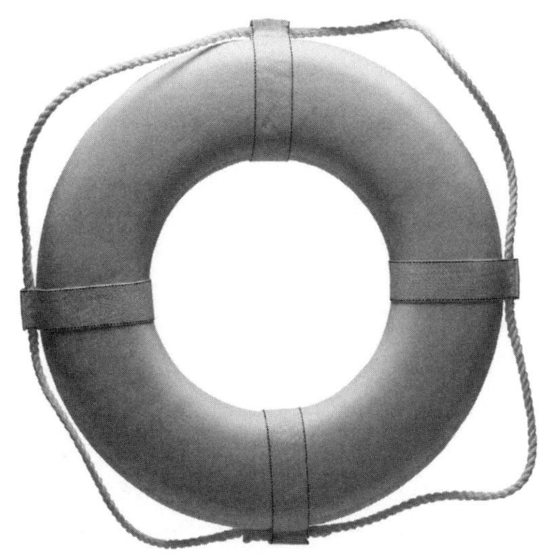

One of a small business owner's biggest fears is a dispute with the federal, state, or local government: either the dreaded IRS audit or a lawsuit that alleges a violation of a statute or local ordinance.

Make no mistake—a good legal compliance program is an absolute necessity if you are to succeed in business because one small mistake, however innocent, can grow out of control in a hurry.

I recently was contacted by a company that had incorporated in Delaware in 1977. The company had originally done business in Pennsylvania, and it had registered with the authorities there as a "foreign" company, as it should have done. In 1990, the owner of the company (and its sole employee) moved his residence to Connecticut and wanted to move his business there as well. He retained an attorney in Pennsylvania, who filed all the forms necessary for his company to "shut down" its legal presence in that state.

When he arrived in Connecticut, he decided to save some money in legal fees by "doing it himself." He registered his company with the state tax authorities but neglected to register his Delaware corporation as a "foreign company" with the Secretary of State's office. Fourteen years later, he wanted to sue a deadbeat customer, but when the case came to court, it came to light that he had never registered his Delaware corporation with the Secretary of State's office and was denied access to the Connecticut courts until such time as he registered.

Even though he had diligently paid all his taxes to Connecticut since 1990, the Secretary of State's office imposed a total of $25,000 in interest and penalties for his operating an "illegal business" in Connecticut for fourteen years. While we were able to negotiate a lower amount with the state because he clearly was able to prove that his was a good faith mistake (his paying taxes for fourteen years certainly did help) and was not intended to cheat the taxpayers, the final settlement

was still a sizeable one, and he is currently in the process of paying it out over ten years.

There are two ways the government ties into your small business—they impose taxes on your business's income and transactions, and they adopt regulations with which you must comply. A good business lawyer (see Chapter 11) can help you through the maze of taxes and regulations that apply specifically to your business and can help you develop compliance programs that will keep Uncle Sam from knocking on your door with his hand out.

Income Taxes

Like individuals, businesses have to pay income taxes. These taxes are imposed by the federal government, by most states, and by some local governments. So, for example, businesses located in New York City must pay income taxes to the federal, state, and city governments.

The income tax, in principle, is extremely easy to understand. Your business gets revenue from selling products and services, you deduct from that revenue your business expenses, depreciation, and other "deductions" and "credits" the government allows you to take, and you pay taxes at a specified rate on your "net income" or "taxable income"—essentially whatever's left over.

There's only one problem. As one of my tax law professors in law school once put it, "If the only purpose of the income tax was to raise money for the Government, the Internal Revenue Code would be only ten pages long, and your annual tax return would fit on the back of a post card." In the United States, we tend to use the income tax as a tool for social engineering—encouraging certain types of behavior and discouraging others.

For example, take the deduction for the interest on your home mortgage. Interest on a home mortgage is deductible, as you know, but the rent you pay to your landlord if you don't own a home is not deductible. Why? Both are "housing expenses," and you could make a pretty good case that "housing expenses," regardless of the form of payment, should be either 100 percent deductible or 100 percent not deductible.

That's not the way the system works; because we want to encourage home ownership in the United States, we allow homeowners to deduct interest on their mortgages as an incentive and deny deductions to renters as a way to "incentivize" them to buy houses.

There are thousands of such examples of social engineering in the federal Internal Revenue Code, which is why it is more than 10,000 pages long, requiring another 30,000 pages of dense regulations to explain how it works.

There is absolutely no way you can know everything about the income tax, and there is absolutely no way I or anyone else can make it simple for you to understand. A CPA/tax lawyer friend of mind put it very well: "When you're talking about the Tax Code, the only way you can be 100 percent sure you are not making any mistakes is to read it out loud, verbatim, without leaving any words out." Within each section of the Tax Code, there are rules, followed by exceptions, followed by exceptions to the exceptions, followed by exceptions to the exceptions to the exceptions, and so forth . . . until you get to the very end of the Section, where there's a clause that begins "notwithstanding any of the foregoing . . . ," and off you go again.

Having said all that, there are only two ways you can get into trouble with income taxes: either you don't report all of the income you've earned during the year, or you take too many deductions.

Under-Reporting Income

The IRS gets really nasty when you fail to report all the income you've made in a given year. The surest way to under-report your income each year is to keep sloppy records and lose things left and right. When you run a business, money comes into your possession in one of three ways: people either pay you cash, write you checks, or pay by credit card (if you have registered as a merchant with one of the major credit card companies). Here are some tips and suggestions for making sure every penny of income in your business is accounted for:

» Avoid payments in cash wherever possible—where you must accept cash, give a written receipt with a carbon copy and keep the carbon copy in a separate file for "cash receipts."
» Keep a separate checking account for your business and make sure all business checks are deposited into the business account, not your personal account.
» When you are depositing several checks at once, record each deposit separately, along with the name of the customer or client that paid you.
» Keep merchant card statements that you receive from credit card issuers each month.

Taking Too Many Deductions

When you have your own business, as the saying goes, "life is deductible." Well, not really. Since small business owners are more likely than other folks to fool around with their deductible expenses, you are more likely to be audited by the IRS than, for example, an executive with a large corporation. There is absolutely nothing wrong with claiming every

legitimate deduction to which you and your business are entitled. There is a two-step process you need to follow to make sure you're taking every deduction you're entitled to without getting too greedy.

Know Exactly What You Can and Cannot Deduct

Since many accountants either don't know you well enough to know precisely what you can and cannot deduct and since many accountants are conservative types who do everything "by the book" and will not let you deduct a dollar unless you can produce ten notarized receipts from the people you paid, it is up to you to learn as much as you can about the various types of deductions and tell your accountant what you think you are entitled to deduct without leaving the decision up to him or her. For a thorough listing of the most common small business deductions, check out 101 Tax Loopholes for Small Business, an audio CD program by Diane Kennedy, CPA, of Phoenix, Arizona (www.taxloopholes.com).

Keep Records Backing Up Every Deduction You Take

Nobody likes keeping records, but here's an easy way to keep track of deductible items:

- Keep a file folder for each deductible expense—when you pay cash for these things, keep the receipt and put it in the folder.
- When writing checks, put an asterisk (*) next to each check you think is paying for a deductible item—that way, at the end of the year, you will have to pull only those checks marked by an asterisk in your check register.
- Keep copies of all of your credit card statements and highlight deductible items with a yellow marker.

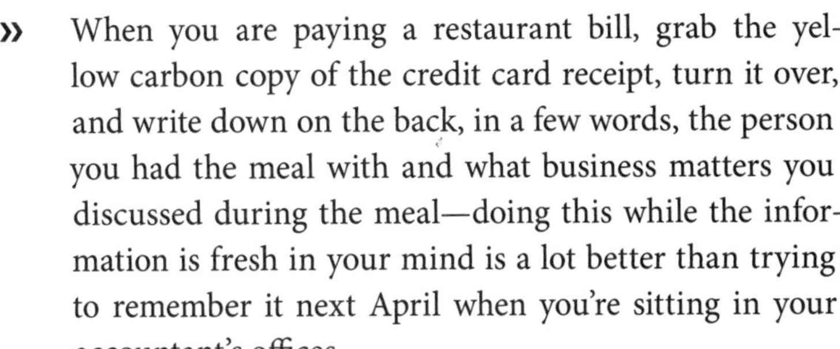

- When you are paying a restaurant bill, grab the yellow carbon copy of the credit card receipt, turn it over, and write down on the back, in a few words, the person you had the meal with and what business matters you discussed during the meal—doing this while the information is fresh in your mind is a lot better than trying to remember it next April when you're sitting in your accountant's offices.
- Keep a mileage log in your car and write down (1) the exact miles your car traveled each day (look at the odometer and subtract yesterday's mileage) and (2) the approximate percentage of time you were driving on business that day—that way, it will be a lot easier to calculate the mileage deduction at the end of the year.

The IRS publishes more than 100 "audit guides" containing "rules of thumb" and "benchmarks" that it uses when determining the appropriate amount of deductions that a self-employed person in that business can legitimately take. Someone who takes lots of deductions in excess of the "benchmark" for his or her business is going to have a lot of explaining to do. Find out if there's an Audit Guide for your business (you can research this information by going to www.irs.gov or to a tax information Web site such as www.wwwebtax.com and searching for "audit guides") and get yourself a copy so you can determine if your deductions are in line with the IRS's expectations.

Withholding, Self-Employment, and Estimated Taxes

When you are self-employed, no one is standing over your shoulder making sure you are deducting taxes from your pay

each week. You are required to withhold income taxes and pay self-employment taxes each year. Basically, self-employment tax is the same amount you would have had withheld from your paycheck for Social Security, federal unemployment taxes, and Medicare taxes if you had been employed by someone else and earned the same amount of income in the form of wages. Because the government worries that you may not be disciplined enough to keep enough cash in reserve to pay your taxes when they're due, they require you to estimate your tax liability and pay in quarterly installments—on April 15, June 15, September 15, and January 15 of each year.

One of the most painful experiences you will have as a self-employed person is writing those huge—and, I mean HUGE—checks to the government four times a year. But paying estimated taxes isn't so bad . . . as long as you have the money in your checking account to pay them with. If your records show that you owe the government $10,000 for the current quarter and you only have $3,000 in your checking account because you went on a wild spending spree to celebrate your fortieth birthday, you are in a lot of trouble. The IRS does not like to wait for what it considers "its" money.

Here's the best way to avoid problems with estimated taxes. When you open your business, ask your bank to open two separate checking accounts for you. The first account will be your "operating account"—this is where you will deposit checks from customers and write checks to pay your suppliers. The second account will be your "tax account"—nothing goes into this account except your quarterly estimated tax payments.

At the end of each month, total up all of the gross income you received in your business during the month, calculate 40 percent of that amount, write a check to yourself for that 40 percent amount, and deposit that check into the "tax account." Then, forget that the money is even there—learn to operate your business on the 60 percent that remains in the "operating account." Then, when each quarterly estimated tax payment is due, write checks to the IRS and your state tax authority from the "tax account."

Now, you may be saying—40 percent? Isn't the highest federal tax rate only 35 percent? You are of course correct, but don't forget state and local income taxes. In working with a lot of clients who are in the highest federal income tax bracket (currently 35 percent), I find that withholding 40 percent of your income for taxes is a good "rule of thumb." If anything, you are overwithholding slightly, which is a good thing. If you overwithhold, leave the excess money in the "tax account" and save it for the next estimated tax payment because you never know what could happen.

Estate and "Death" Taxes

One of the biggest problems facing a closely held family business in the United States is the impact of estate, death, and inheritance taxes when the company founder dies. Too frequently, the heirs of a deceased small business owner—who are only too willing to assume responsibility for the business's future success—are forced to sell the business outside the family in order to come up with the cash to pay a gigantic tax bill (the federal estate tax alone can be as high as 55 percent of the estate's value).

One of the planning techniques used to avoid this result is the family limited partnership (FLP), in which the company founder transfers his or her shares to a newly formed limited partnership in exchange for the general partner's interest in the limited partnership. Here's how it works.

The founder's spouse, children, and other heirs become the limited partners of the limited partnership for a nominal

capital contribution, usually $100. The limited partnership agreement of a FLP provides that the lion's share of all partnership distributions—usually 99 percent—are allocated to the limited partners, with the result that the limited partners' interests grow substantially over time. When the general partner dies (hopefully not soon after the FLP is formed), the bulk of the stock owned by the FLP has been transferred tax-free to the deceased's heirs, who now own substantially all of the FLP's economic interests. The FLP, if structured properly, has the additional tax benefit that persons owning a minority interest in the partnership may qualify for a substantial discount when it comes time to value the interest for tax purposes.

FLPs are extremely complex to set up, and the IRS is likely to audit your FLP aggressively if even slight mistakes are made. Do not attempt to set up a FLP without the assistance of an extremely good attorney who specializes in "trusts and estates."

Sales Taxes

With one or two exceptions, just about every state imposes a "sales tax" on retail transactions—that is, sales to the ultimate consumer of a product or service. Unlike Canada and most European nations, the United States does not have a "value-added tax" or "general services tax"—this is a sales tax that applies to both wholesale and retail transactions. In the United States, sales taxes apply only to retail transactions and are imposed by the states (and sometimes by local governments), not the federal government.

In most states, you are required to collect and pay sales taxes and file sales tax returns on a quarterly basis. Failure to determine the correct amount or file a return on time can lead to a sales tax audit, which is probably one of the ugliest events you will ever have to go through in your life.

Sales taxes are fairly easy to calculate. You merely total up the retail sales your business has generated during the quarter, multiply by the sales tax percentage, and write a check for the resulting amount to your state government. There are a number of ways you can get into trouble with sales taxes, as follows.

Thinking Your Service Is Not Taxable When It in Fact Is

Most states levy sales taxes on the retail sales of goods, but a growing number of states (desperate for revenue and unwilling to raise their citizens' income taxes for fear of retribution at the polls) impose sales taxes on services as well. In states that impose sales taxes on services, there frequently are a host of exceptions from the tax (professional services, for example—there's something just downright un-American about taxing somebody's legal fees), and it's easy to make mistakes.

Take management consulting, for example. Quite a number of states tax management consulting services. You are a "business coach" that helps entrepreneurs and business owners work through their personal issues as a manager. You don't consider yourself a management consultant, and McKinsey & Co. would certainly never hire you to do what you do for folks. Yet, you may be considered a "management consultant" under your state's sales tax law.

A nice collection of the sales tax laws of all fifty states and summaries of what's taxable and not taxable in each state can be found at the Web site of the U.S. Sales Tax Institute (www.salestaxinstitute.com), but the best advice here is to talk to a tax lawyer or accountant and make sure that you know exactly which of your products and services are subject to sales tax and which aren't.

Thinking Your Transaction Is Wholesale When It's Really Retail

In almost all states, sales taxes apply only to retail transactions; wholesale transactions are exempt from sales tax. But how do you know if a transaction is really wholesale?

Let's say a customer orders 500 widgets from you. He swears that he is buying them for resale (in other words, at wholesale), but in fact he is using them in his own business, which makes your sale a retail transaction subject to sales tax. The best protection here is to obtain a Resale Tax Certificate from the buyer, basically an affidavit in which the buyer certifies in writing that his purchase of product from you is wholesale, not retail in nature. That way, if the state ever audits you for sales tax, all you have to do is produce the Certificate, and you're off the hook—the state will go after your buyer, who is now liable for signing a fraudulent affidavit. The Resale Exemption Certificate available at www.cliffennico.com is a typical form of Resale Tax Certificate, but your state tax authority will probably require that you use their form, usually available as a free download from their Web site. (For a list of Web sites of the fifty state tax authorities, go to www.natptax.com, the Web site of the National Association of Tax Professionals; go to their home page and click on "state information," then click on your state on the U.S. map that will pop up on your screen.)

Thinking Your Transaction Is Interstate Rather Than Local

Sales between residents of different states are not subject to sales tax. This is because of a provision in the U.S. Constitution prohibiting the states from taxing interstate commerce. But when is a sale truly interstate?

Let's say, for example, you have offices in three different states. Someone from one of these states calls you and orders a product or service. Rather than refer the customer to your local branch office in his state, you fulfill the order yourself. Even though the order shipped from your warehouse, the fact that the customer resides in a state where you maintain a branch office means that you are required to collect and pay that state's sales tax on the transaction.

What about sales made over the Internet, you may ask? This is probably one of the hottest topics in tax law right now because a lot of states are hurting for revenue and feel they are losing billions of dollars in sales taxes each year to Internet transactions. More than twenty states have adopted legislation in support of the Streamlined Sales Tax Project (SSTP), which requires out-of-state vendors (such as eBay sellers) to charge sales tax when selling to in-state consumers. A 1992 U.S. Supreme Court decision forbids states from enforcing the SSTP, but legislation is pending in Congress to reverse this decision and allow states to pursue out-of-state vendors who don't comply with the SSTP. For further information, check out the NetChoice Coalition (www.NetChoice.org), a grass-roots organization devoted to fighting sales taxes on interstate commerce.

Each state has its own rules on whether a transaction is "in-state" or "interstate" for purposes of the sales tax, but the rules are all over the map and impossible to simplify for the general reader. It is a good idea to be very conservative here; if you live in Iowa and you sell something over the Internet to a customer in Iowa, you should collect and pay sales tax on that transaction, even though your Web site is hosted on a computer server in California.

Use Taxes

A while back I received the following e-mail from a client: "Back in December 2001 I bought some jewelry over the Internet from a company in Germany as a holiday present for my

wife. Last month I received a nasty notice from my state tax department saying that I owe tax on that purchase, together with interest and penalties from 2001. The bill comes to several hundred dollars. I wrote back and said this wasn't a business purchase, but they said it doesn't matter. I still have to pay the tax. Can this be possible?"

It looks like this fellow received an unwelcome visit from the Ghost of Christmas Past—one that many business owners and well-to-do individuals will be receiving in the months ahead as state and local governments try to squeeze more revenue out of tax bases that are not growing.

The culprit here is something called a "use tax," which most states have. A use tax is the flip side of a sales tax—you pay it on things you buy and consume in your business from vendors that did not charge you sales tax. Just like a sales tax, you don't pay it on your inventory and other stuff you buy for resale. So, for example, if you buy a computer that you intend to use in your business from an out-of-state vendor that didn't charge you sales tax, you have to pay use tax to your state for the privilege of consuming or "using" the computer within your state.

Now, some of you are probably saying: "Hey, wait a minute! If the states can do that, they're taxing interstate commerce, and I thought that was illegal." Well, not necessarily. Technically, a use tax does not tax the sale or transfer of goods from one state to another. It taxes the use or consumption of the goods within the state, which is perfectly legal. If you are actually using the goods in another state (this is highly unlikely), you probably have a defense to the state's attempt to collect the tax.

In many states, use taxes apply not only to business purchases but personal, individual purchases as well. Most people are unaware of this tax and with good reason. State and local governments have been lax in enforcing their use taxes because they don't have an adequate way to monitor whether people are buying things without paying sales taxes (if you paid a sales tax, you don't pay use tax on top of it). I think what happened to this client is that the German company issued a customs declaration when it shipped the jewelry to him, and the "declared value" on the customs slip eventually became part of the public government record that his state tax department was able to track down. Clearly, he has to pay the tax and keep his fingers crossed that the state doesn't use this as a pretext for a "use tax" audit of his purchases over the last several years.

Personal Property Taxes

In addition to sales and use taxes, some states impose a personal property tax based on a "mill rate." Like a real estate tax, you pay so many dollars of tax for each $1,000 of taxable personal property your business owns.

In some states, the personal property tax applies only to cars, boats, and other vehicles that have to be registered. Other states tax businesses only on their machinery, equipment, and other property that you depreciate for tax purposes. Still other states extend their tax to cover supplies and other items (yes, even including paper clips) that you use or consume in your business. If your state or local government has a personal property tax, you should check with your accountant to determine if your business uses any of the types of property to which the tax applies.

If your business owns property that is subject to the tax, however, it won't matter where you bought the item or whether or not you paid sales taxes when you bought it. You will have to pay the tax.

The "Contractor" Who Is Really an Employee

A couple of years ago, a federal court required the mighty Microsoft Corporation to offer employee benefits to people who signed agreements saying they were independent contractors (ICs).

Microsoft had classified a group of temporary workers as ICs, calling them "freelancers" or "permatemps." The workers signed contracts agreeing to be responsible for all federal and state taxes, Social Security and Medicare tax, insurance, and other benefits. The IRS subsequently reclassified the ICs as employees, primarily on the basis that they were working at Microsoft full-time, didn't work for anyone else, and Microsoft controlled and directed them in performing their duties for Microsoft.

Then some of the workers sued Microsoft to get employee benefits that they would have enjoyed if they had been properly classified as employees. These benefits included participation in a savings plan, which was a 401(k) plan, and a stock option plan that allowed participants to buy Microsoft stock at 85 percent of the value of the stock on certain dates. A federal appeals court sided with the "permatemps," even though they had signed agreements with Microsoft waiving any right to benefits, ruling that the only reason the workers were not on the Microsoft payroll was because of Microsoft's unlawful purpose of avoiding employer payroll and benefit costs.

The Microsoft case makes it clear that courts are only too willing to throw out even well-drafted IC agreements if, based on a review of all the "facts and circumstances," the person signing the contract is treated as an employee. Because many home-based businesses cannot afford to hire employees and must rely on relationships with independent contractors, a review of the rules distinguishing employees from ICs is in order.

First, the basics. Anyone who works for your business (other than a partner) is either an employee or an IC.

An employee is someone over whose activities you have some degree of control. You not only tell the employee what to do and when to do it, but also how to do it and in what order of priority. If someone is your employee, you must:

- Withhold federal, state, and (sometimes) local income taxes
- Make payments to the federal and state unemployment compensation programs
- Pay federal and state payroll taxes
- Issue a W-2 to the employee within thirty days after the end of each calendar year

Everyone else who works for your business is an IC. Take me, for example. I'm an attorney with more than 100 clients, none of which account for more than 5 percent of my time in any given month. I do not work fifty or more hours a week for any one client on a regular basis. You can tell me what you want done and when you need it done, and you can put limits on how much you will spend to have it done. But you can't tell me where to work, you can't hover over me every minute making sure I'm doing it, and you can't insist I put other clients on hold to do your work immediately (although Lord knows some clients try). If I do work for multiple clients at the same time, you have nothing to say about it as long as I deliver the goods on time. I deliver an invoice at the end of each month, and you pay it in thirty days or you receive a visit from my cousin Vito. It is highly unlikely the IRS or anyone else would argue that I was your employee merely because I drafted a couple of contracts for you.

If someone is an IC, you don't have to withhold taxes, pay payroll taxes, or contribute to unemployment compensation,

although if you pay an IC more than $600 in any calendar year you are supposed to deliver IRS Form 1099 to him or her within thirty days after the end of the calendar year.

So how do you tell the difference between an employee and an IC? The short answer is . . . nobody can tell you with 100 percent certainty if an individual is an employee or an IC. From 1987 to 1996, IRS auditors used a set of twenty "guidelines" to help tell the difference, but the auditors were free to apply and weigh the guidelines pretty much as they saw fit. Of course, they did. Anyone the IRS agents saw as they walked through your office was an employee, and you had the burden of proving otherwise.

In 1996, the IRS issued a training manual for its auditors simplifying the rules for distinguishing between employees and ICs. While the manual doesn't have the force of law, the IRS expects its auditors to follow it and has begun training them to do so. The IRS manual provides the best guidance the IRS has ever made public on how to classify workers and suggests a kinder, gentler attitude by the IRS on this issue.

The keystone to employee status is "control." Does the company have the right to control a worker's activity? If it does, that worker is likely to be classified as an employee. If it doesn't, the worker is likely to be classified as an IC. The IRS has instructed its auditors to look at three areas to determine whether a hiring firm has the right to control a worker's activity:

- Behavioral control
- Financial control
- Relationship of the parties

There is no magic number or "point system" to determine whether a worker is an employee or an IC. All that is required for a worker to be considered an IC is that the factors showing lack of control outweigh those that indicate control.

Behavioral Control

Behavioral control means how you and your workers deal with each other on the job. Be careful how you give "instructions" to your workers. If you are telling your workers when to do the work, where to do the work, what tools or equipment to use, where to purchase supplies or services, what work must be performed by a specific person, and what order or sequences to follow in doing the work, the workers are likely to be classified as employees. If, however, your instructions cover only the end results a worker must achieve and his or her "deadline," they are perfectly consistent with IC status.

A suggestion about how work is to be performed does not constitute the right to control. However, if complying with suggestions is mandatory or the worker would suffer adverse consequences if he or she doesn't comply (such as termination or failure to receive more work), then the suggestions will be treated as "instructions," and the worker will be deemed an employee.

Providing a worker with periodic or ongoing training about procedures to be followed or methods to be used on a job is a strong indicator of employee status. A short orientation or information meeting about your company policies, however, will not jeopardize the worker's IC status. Similarly, it is okay to evaluate the quality of an IC's final work product, but you should not use an evaluation system to measure compliance with performance standards concerning the details of how the work is performed.

Financial Control

Because employees usually don't make investments in the equipment or facilities they use on a job, a worker who has a significant investment in equipment or facilities is likely to

be classified as an IC. An IC can even lease equipment from the hiring firm provided he or she pays fair rental value.

Similarly, a worker who pays his or her own business expenses out of pocket is likely to be classified as an IC, even if those expenses are ultimately reimbursed by the hiring firm. At least some expenses, however, must be unreimbursed. The IRS is particularly impressed by fixed ongoing costs that are incurred regardless of whether work is currently being performed, such as office rent.

Paying a worker a flat fee for an entire job is very strong evidence he or she is an IC, especially if the worker's expenses are not reimbursed. The worker runs the risk of losing money if the job takes longer or expenses are higher than anticipated, but he or she can also earn a windfall if the work is done quickly with lower expenses than anticipated. Such an opportunity to earn a profit or suffer a loss is a hallmark of IC status.

In contrast, paying an IC an hourly wage makes him or her look like an employee, unless hourly rates are customary in the IC's industry. Most lawyers and bookkeepers, for example, bill by the hour, so paying your lawyer an hourly rate should not cause him or her to be classified as an IC.

Relationship of the Parties

What the IRS is looking for here is how you and the worker perceive your relationship with one another. If you and a worker intended to create an IC relationship instead of an employee relationship, you likely will not have the right to control the worker.

A written agreement describing the worker as an IC is good evidence that you and the worker intended to create an IC relationship. As Microsoft found out to its chagrin, however, even a well-drafted IC agreement will not protect you if your intent was to "paper over" an employee relationship.

In my small business seminars, I constantly come across seasonal service businesses—such as landscapers and building contractors—who ask the following question: "I've got a guy who works for me. He works sixty hours a week, but only during the summer. The rest of the year he collects unemployment. He doesn't work for anyone else. If I get him to sign a contract saying he's not an employee, will that hold up?" Almost certainly, the answer is "no."

Providing a worker with employee-type benefits such as health insurance, sick leave, paid vacations, or pension benefits is evidence that you intended to create an employment relationship. Also, you should never file a W-2 form for a worker you intend to treat as an IC.

Employees are typically hired for an indefinite period; they continue to work as long as their employers need their services. ICs, on the other hand, work on a project-by-project basis. Make sure your IC contract clearly specifies the project and states clearly that the contract terminates when the project ends. Where this is not possible, make sure the contract has a definite expiration date.

Finally, a factor IRS auditors look at is whether the services a worker performs are key to the hiring firm's regular business. For example, an accounting firm is less likely to supervise and control a painter it hires to paint its offices than a bookkeeper it hires to work on its regular client accounts. However, the bookkeeper still may be classified as an IC if the firm can show that he or she was a specialist hired to help with especially difficult or unusual work.

Basically, you can't define an employee with 100 percent precision, but you know one when you see one. As a colleague of mine put it, "If it walks like a duck, talks like a duck, waddles like a duck, and works like a dog, don't try telling the IRS it's an independent contractor." If you are not sure whether a particular worker is likely to be classified as an employee or

an IC, you should review the matter with a competent attorney who specializes in labor and employment matters.

Government Regulation: The Need to Get Involved

One of your first challenges as a business owner is to find out about the state and local regulations that apply to your business and make sure you comply with them. If you are in the business of refilling people's toner cartridges, are there environmental laws saying how you must dispose of the used toner? If you are in the check-cashing business, must you obtain a license from your state banking department before you open your doors? If you are baking cookies out of your home kitchen (as part of a business), must you redo your bathroom to make it compliant with federal Americans With Disabilities Act (ADA) requirements? (A client of mine was recently forced to do just that.)

Government regulations are all over the board, and there's no way I can summarize them all in a single book. The best advice here is:

- Subscribe to publications and newsletters in your state that announce new business regulations. A list of state government publications is usually maintained by your state government library and is available online. To find your state government library's Web site, go to the Library of Congress State and Local Government Information Web site at www.loc.gov/global/library/statelib.html.
- Work closely with a small business lawyer who is familiar with your business and can keep you posted on new developments in state law and regulation that will affect your business.

- Get politically involved. If your state legislature is considering new laws that will adversely affect your business, don't just sit back and accept it as "Kismet"; call the state legislators in your district and express your concerns.
- Find a lobbyist who specializes in business regulation in your state and develop a relationship with him or her. Since most lobbyists are required to register as such, contact your state Secretary of State's office (the Web site name is usually www.sos.state.yourstateabbreviation.us) and ask for a list of lobbyists in your area.

Remember that great slogan from the 1960s: "If you aren't part of the system, you are part of the problem." Get involved, or get steamrolled.

CHAPTER 7

SPOUSES AND EX-SPOUSES: POTENTIAL BUSINESS "THIEVES"?

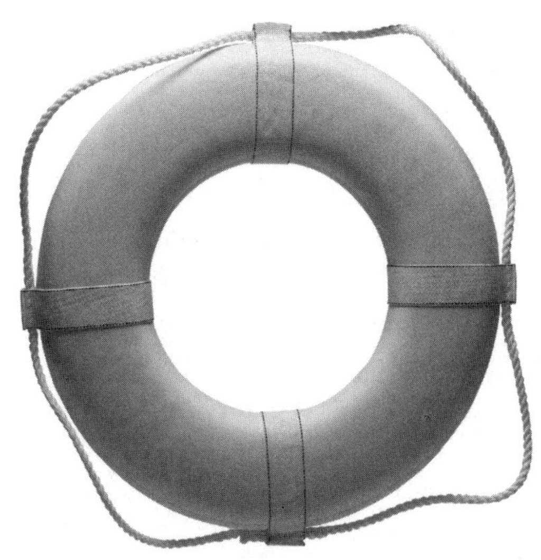

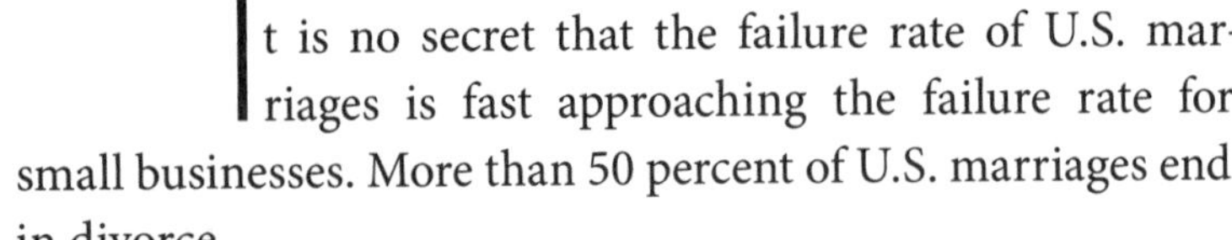

It is no secret that the failure rate of U.S. marriages is fast approaching the failure rate for small businesses. More than 50 percent of U.S. marriages end in divorce.

You may be thinking: “Wait a minute! My spouse has nothing to do with my business. He or she doesn’t even work for a living. You’re telling me that if we get divorced, he or she can steal my business?” Well, probably not all of it. The family court judge will probably let you keep some ownership in your business so you have an incentive to keep working and pay all the alimony, child support, and other cash goodies your nonworking spouse will likely get.

Divorce courts are notoriously sympathetic to a nonworking spouse. If your spouse does not have an independent means of financially supporting him- or herself and your children (and increasingly, even if he or she does), a divorce court is likely to award your spouse a substantial chunk of your assets if you divorce or separate. If, like many entrepreneurs, the bulk of your personal assets is tied up in your business, and your company stock, options, or 401(k) plan assets constitute the major part of your personal wealth, what do you think the court will award your spouse in a divorce settlement? Your frequent-flier miles?

Once upon a time, the law was simple, at least in most states. If you owned a business and all of your stock was held in your name alone, it was the end of the story. If you and your spouse divorced, all assets went to the spouse in whose name the asset was legally registered. The only exception was in so-called community property states, such as California and a handful of other states in the southwestern United States whose history can be traced back to the Spanish or Mexican legal system. In “community property” states, judges routinely divided a couple’s assets neatly in half and awarded one-half to each spouse.

Over the last twenty years, however, divorce courts in just about every state have been awarded broad powers to look at all the assets of a divorcing couple, regardless of their legal ownership, and cherry-pick the assets that will most likely support a nonworking spouse with minor children. This is called "equitable distribution." What it means in practice is that if all of your wealth is tied up in your company's stock, options, or other securities, a court has the power to award to your ex-spouse up to 50 percent and, in some cases, more of your ownership interest in your business.

Why this change in attitude? There are two reasons; the first of which is historical. Once upon a time, most Americans worked for someone else. Their personal wealth was tied up in a salary and other cash compensation (such as an annual bonus) or perhaps an inheritance from a wealthy relative. Today, a significant portion of many Americans' wealth—even those who still labor for others—consists of equity and other forms of contingent compensation such as stock options. It is not uncommon for many start-up companies to pay their senior management employees exclusively in stock and options, which gives rise to the jokes about CEOs who raid the vending machines at night and live on Diet Coke and peanut butter sandwiches during the first year of operations. To base a divorce settlement on just the cash component of such a person's compensation is, in the eyes of many divorce judges, unfair to the person's spouse.

The second reason has to do with a shift in legal thinking about divorce. Once upon a time, the goal of divorce settlements and awards was to maintain a nonworking spouse economically, in the manner in which he or she had become accustomed. In other words, the settlement looked to your past earnings and gave a divorced spouse enough to keep them going based on what the spouse had expected during the marriage. If your settlement was enough to feed, clothe,

house, and educate your ex-spouse and minor children, based on your earnings during the marriage, that was usually considered enough.

Over time, divorce law has adopted a new and quite different principle—that a spouse has lost not only current income in a divorce, but also the opportunity to participate in the future income and wealth of his or her working spouse. In other words, divorce settlements today are forward-looking rather than backward-looking. The idea now is not merely to "maintain" the ex-spouse, but to compensate them for the income and wealth they would have had if the marriage had not dissolved. Courts in most states are now highly receptive to the idea that spouses—especially nonworking spouses with no independent sources of income—should be entitled to a piece of their working spouses' future earnings and wealth.

There is probably only one thing worse than divorce, and that is waking up one morning to find out you are now working eighty or more hours each week for your undeserving "ex," who knows as much about your business as you do about the subatomic particles that make up the neutron of the atom. If you quit your job to avoid this painful situation, you not only lose your job, but are also in violation of a court order and can be thrown in jail. If you file for bankruptcy in the hope of avoiding your obligation to your ex-spouse, you open yourself up to the possibility that your spouse or other potential thieves will be awarded all of your stock in the bankruptcy settlement. Even worse, you may find out that your undeserving "ex," who cannot stand the very sight of you (and vice versa) and owns 50 percent or more of your stock, now wants to work for your company and second-guess your every business judgment as a full-fledged partner in the enterprise. And you thought that indentured servitude was illegal in America!

Protecting your business against an ex-spouse in divorce proceedings is a particularly tricky matter. If a divorce court even suspects that an agreement or arrangement between you and your spouse was not 100 percent fair and evenhanded, it usually has the power to disregard your agreement or arrangement and do what it darn well pleases. In order to protect your business, you must come up with a way to make sure your future or present spouse will be protected in the event of divorce without getting his or her hands on your business.

As with all other solutions to protecting your business, the time to protect yourself is before the damage is done—in this case, before you and your spouse walk down the aisle. Once you've reached the point where you are no longer talking to your spouse, it's too late.

Of course, it's not easy to discuss such a delicate subject with your spouse while the bloom of romance is still fresh. Even broaching the subject could increase the level of tension in your relationship. But do it you must. If you are like most entrepreneurs, you have built your business before you even have time to pursue relationships, so your future spouse should (and hopefully will) understand your priorities. If this is a second, third, or fourth relationship for either of you, the subject should be much easier to broach, since there is the added need to protect spouses and children from prior relationships.

There is a tradeoff in discussing these issues with your present or future spouse—the more aggressively you try to protect your business, the more likely you are to alienate your spouse and destroy a beautiful relationship. Similarly, the more you avoid unpleasant discussions with your spouse in an effort protect your relationship, the more you put your business at risk should your marriage dissolve. Of all the things you need to do to protect your business, the matters covered in this chapter are by far the most difficult.

It may sound cynical, but I've always believed that a frank discussion of the need to protect your business against

outsiders is a good way to find out what your future mate most desires in you. As one entrepreneur friend of mine put it, "If you can't talk frankly about money with someone, that someone is not right for you, and you should walk away from the relationship. If it's the right person, your soul mate, then you are the attraction for them, not your business, your money, or anything else." While I agree generally with this sentiment, I wouldn't take it too far. If you stick a one-sided agreement in front of your present or future spouse and demand they sign it as a demonstration of affection or loyalty, I won't be surprised if they tell you to take your agreement and stick it somewhere else. This is a delicate matter and must be handled delicately. But above all, it must be handled somehow. Here are some suggestions that might—if handled the right way—protect your business and preserve your romantic relationship at the same time.

The Buy-Sell Agreement

The most effective way to ensure that your spouse will not steal your business is the "buy-sell" agreement, discussed at length in Chapter 8. In a buy-sell agreement, the founders of a business agree that if certain specified things happen to a founder (death, disability, bankruptcy, withdrawal from the business, and so forth), the other founders will buy the departing founder's stake in the company for a price that's agreed on beforehand.

Most buy-sell agreements contain an "involuntary transfer" clause, specifying what will happen should the stock of one of the parties be seized by a creditor, a court, or other third party without the consent or approval of the party concerned. If you think about it for a minute, the award of one-half or more of your stock to an ex-spouse in a divorce proceeding is just such an "involuntary transfer." Yet, to my knowledge, very few buy-sell agreements provide for the divorce of one of the company founders and the subsequent award of a significant portion of that founder's stock to an ex-spouse who is an "outsider" to the agreement. If you visit www.cliffennico.com, you will find an "Involuntary Transfer" clause from a typical LLC buy-sell agreement that includes a specific reference to the "termination of the marriage" of one of the company founders. Buy-sell agreements can be very tricky to draft, and it is best to have a local attorney put one together for you rather than your trying to do it yourself. The total cost should be less than $1,000, unless you and your partners ask for a lot of "bells and whistles."

The beauty of the buy-sell agreement is that the present or future spouse need not be a party to the agreement. In other words, the founders of the business can agree, among themselves, to buy any shares that may be involuntarily transferred to a spouse, and the spouse need not agree to the arrangement. This avoids the unpleasantness of having to bring up the whole subject of disposition of assets on divorce at a point in time where the couple is just beginning to know each other. Of course, there is no guarantee a divorce court will approve such an arrangement unless it is eminently fair and equitable to the aggrieved spouse. If the agreement is properly drafted, the divorce court will go along with the arrangement and allow the founders (other than the divorcing founder) to buy out the spouse at the agreed price. After all, given the choice, a person who is not familiar with his or her spouse's business will almost always prefer cash today to stock in a company with unlimited (but highly speculative) future potential.

For the buy-sell agreement to work, the purchase price must be a fair one. An agreement among the founders to buy the shares of a founder's spouse for $1.00 each, for example, is not likely to be upheld by the courts if the fair market value of

the shares is substantially in excess of that amount. A divorce court is more likely to enforce the agreement if the purchase price truly represents the fair market value of the shares being purchased. The fairest arrangement would be one in which the purchase price is determined by a committee of three "appraisers" (who may be investment bankers, accountants, or other financial experts)—one selected by the company, one selected by the divorced spouse who has been awarded shares in the company, and the third selected by the other two appraisers. (This approach, incidentally, is often referred to as a "Three Stooges" appraisal—probably because of what happens when these three strangers meet for the first time behind closed doors and attempt to come up with a fair value for the company's shares.) With such an approach, it is important to specify the time frames within which a decision must be reached and the person (usually the company) responsible for compensating the three appraisers for their time.

A more complicated approach, but one that is almost certain to win the approval of a divorce court, is the "greater of book or market value" approach. Under this approach, an independent appraiser (or a "Three Stooges" committee as mentioned previously) determines both the book (or liquidation) value of the company and its current fair market value and selects the higher of the two values. While more time-consuming (because two separate valuations are called for, instead of one), this approach has the advantage of securing for a divorced spouse the fair value of a company whose performance has not exactly been stellar. If a company is performing poorly, the book value (the value of the company's assets should the company be liquidated) often more fairly reflects the true value of the company than the fair market or "going concern" value (the value of the company's future potential, often measured as a multiple of the company's pretax earnings over a specified period of time).

Although a properly drafted buy-sell agreement will not require the consent of the spouse or spouse-to-be, the odds of the agreement being enforced by a divorce court will be greatly enhanced if the spouse is given the opportunity to review the agreement prior to marriage, with the assistance of his or her own legal counsel, and an opportunity to sign the agreement on an "acknowledged and agreed" line. An angry spouse will have a more difficult time throwing a buy-sell agreement out of court if he or she has signed it after having been given the opportunity to review it with the assistance of legal counsel.

The Prenuptial Agreement

Prenuptial agreements have gotten a bad rap, especially in the legal press, because people expect too much of them. An agreement between a husband and wife (or a dating couple) that specifies how many kids they are going to have and when, where they are going to live, what religious beliefs they will profess, and how they are going to take care of their respective parents when they can no longer take care of themselves is not likely to last long in a court of law. Such delicate and emotional situations cannot be subject to the cold, analytical, rational analysis of the law (at least not yet—when it comes to the law's ever expanding grip over human relations, never say it will never happen).

Yet, where both parties to a marriage have their own lives—their own businesses, for example, or children from a prior marriage—a prenuptial agreement that is limited in scope to the "economic" aspects of the relationship is almost certain to be enforced. Because an entrepreneur who has given years of his or her life building a business has an obligation to protect that business when he or she embarks upon a romantic relationship, a prenuptial agreement is almost a necessity, one

that the future spouse must be educated to accept as a condition of marriage.

What should the agreement say? Ideally, the agreement should say that the spouse has no interest in the entrepreneur's business and should keep his or her hands off in the event the marriage dissolves. This may not, however, be practical in all situations. Where the entrepreneur has few assets apart from the business, a divorce court is unlikely to tell the aggrieved spouse that he or she is "out of luck" because of a prenuptial agreement.

For a prenuptial agreement to be truly effective, the spouse's agreement not to seize or levy upon the entrepreneur's business assets in the event of a divorce must be conditioned upon the entrepreneur giving up something of equal or greater value. As examples, the entrepreneur could agree:

- » Not to seize or levy upon any asset the spouse brought with him or her to the marriage
- » Not to upset or set aside any trust or any other arrangement the spouse may have set up for the benefit of his or her children from a prior marriage
- » Not to seize or levy upon the stock or other ownership interest in a business the spouse operates at the time of marriage
- » To set up trusts or other arrangements to provide for the welfare of the spouse's children from a prior marriage

In general, the mutual agreement of the spouses to "keep their hands off the other spouse's stuff" should be sufficient, provided there is some arrangement for dividing assets that are created after the marriage takes place. Barring that, the entrepreneur should consider giving up something of real value to the other spouse in exchange for the promise to keep their hands off the entrepreneur's stock and other business assets—a vacation home or yacht, for example.

If you visit www.cliffennico.com, you can find a sample Prenuptial Agreement between two entrepreneurs who have started their own businesses before deciding to marry. Because divorce laws vary widely from state to state, be sure to consult with a lawyer familiar with the laws of your state before using this form.

The Disclaimer Agreement

Perhaps the least effective but most common way business owners try to avoid losing their businesses in a divorce proceeding is the "disclaimer letter" or "disclaimer agreement." On its face, this agreement is a simple letter between a husband and wife in which one states, "in the effect we get a divorce, I will not lay claim to your shares in XYZ Corporation, or any options to acquire shares in XYZ Corporation, and I will not seek to participate in the ownership or management of XYZ Corporation."

It sounds simple enough, doesn't it? Yet if this agreement is not properly drafted, a court is highly likely to throw it out as unenforceable.

The most common mistake in drafting disclaimer agreements is to fail to give your spouse a substantial incentive (called "consideration" in legalese) to sign the agreement. Very often, when a successful entrepreneur starts dating someone seriously, he or she produces a disclaimer agreement at an awkward moment and says, more or less, "Honey, if you love me, I need to know that what I've worked so hard to build all these many years will not be jeopardized by whatever happens to us." The agreement is almost always one-sided: "I agree that I will not try to seize any of your business assets if we divorce."

Nothing is given in exchange except, perhaps, love and affection. Trust me, such an agreement will not stand up in any divorce court in the United States.

A divorce court is granted broad powers to protect nonworking spouses, especially those with children, from unfair agreements and arrangements. If a disclaimer agreement does not give the unfortunate spouse something really valuable in exchange for the promise not to pursue business assets in divorce court, it will not be enforced. One dollar is not enough, nor, surprisingly, is a "mutual" disclaimer agreement, in which each spouse promises not to pursue the business assets of the other. If both spouses own their own businesses at the time such a mutual disclaimer agreement is signed, that may work. But if one spouse is not an entrepreneur and is not likely to become one during the course of the marriage, the divorce court is likely to say that the agreement was "unilateral" (translation: one-sided) and therefore not enforceable.

The only way for a disclaimer agreement to be enforceable is for the spouse to receive something of real value in exchange for their promise not to seize stock or other business assets in the event of divorce.

Here's one way a disclaimer agreement might (I say "might"—no guarantees) be made to work. When an entrepreneur marries, both spouses are concerned that the family home not be subject to seizure by the entrepreneur's business creditors. Yet, the bank that provides the couple with mortgage financing wants both individuals to sign on the dotted line. What usually happens is that both the husband and wife sign the mortgage documents and then, shortly after the closing, the entrepreneur deeds his or her one-half interest in the house to the other spouse for One Dollar "and other good and valuable consideration."

As long as the deed (called a "quitclaim" deed) is delivered and recorded in the real estate records in the town, city, or county where the house is located before the entrepreneur incurs significant business debts, it will usually be enforceable in a court of law. Because the value of one-half of any house is likely to be more than One Dollar, however, there is always the nagging suspicion that if the entrepreneur's business creditors are hurting badly enough, a court might be tempted to set aside the quitclaim deed and let them seize the entrepreneur's one-half interest in the house. Have you ever tried to live in one-half of a house? It ain't easy. Usually the couple is forced to sell the home, pay one-half of the proceeds to the entrepreneur's business creditors, and then use the other half to pay the down payment on another home. Often, the marriage does not survive the process.

One possible way to achieve both spouses' objectives—keep the family home safe from business creditors and protect the business in the event of a nasty divorce proceeding—is for the entrepreneur to transfer his or her one-half interest in the family home in exchange for the spouse's agreement not to seize or levy upon the entrepreneur's business.

Drafting such an agreement is simplicity itself. The entrepreneur deeds his or her one-half interest in the family home to the spouse. The spouse agrees that in the event of divorce, he or she will not seize or levy upon the entrepreneur's stock or other business assets. The whole agreement can be accomplished in a page or two.

There can be no guarantee such an agreement will be enforced in all cases. There are some divorce judges that will go to extreme lengths to protect what they see as "an innocent spouse," no matter what pieces of paper are presented to them. But there is a good chance that a disclaimer agreement given in exchange for an interest in the entrepreneur's personal assets will be upheld in many courts, and it's worth a try. For one thing, the "aggrieved" spouse cannot claim that he or she did not receive anything of value in exchange for giving

up the right to proceed against the entrepreneur's business assets in a divorce proceeding: 50 percent of the value a house in any decent location is a pretty decent chunk of change, no matter where you live.

More importantly, such an agreement makes it more difficult for the court to determine who is wearing the "black hat" and who is wearing the "white hat" in the divorce proceeding. If you cannot—absolutely cannot—avoid a court proceeding, you must make sure that you are not the one wearing the "black hat" when the proceeding begins. At best, you should be the one clearly wearing the "white hat." But if you cannot achieve this, you should try to make sure that both you and the other side are wearing "gray hats" so that the court will be open-minded and listen carefully to what both of you are going to say before making up their mind. A disclaimer agreement that is fair to both sides and gives your spouse something of real value goes a long way toward sending a message to the divorce judge that "I tried to do the right thing here. I may have been a little sloppy, but I'm not the bad guy here. It would be unjust and inequitable to nail me to the wall after I bent over backward to make sure my spouse would be comfortable in the event something bad happened in my business."

That may be enough to get your side of the case heard, which in any divorce proceeding is the most you can ask for.

If you need a sample disclaimer agreement in which an entrepreneur transfers to his spouse one-half of the family home in exchange for a promise from the spouse not to pursue the entrepreneur's business assets in the event of a divorce or separation, visit www.cliffennico.com for the form called Letter from Spouse Disclaiming Interest in Closely Held Business. Because divorce laws vary widely from state to state, be sure to have this form reviewed by a lawyer familiar with the legal rules in your state before you use it.

Be sure to talk this over with your spouse or spouse-to-be before springing any sort of legal agreement on them. Remember there is a tradeoff between protecting your business and preserving your relationship with another human being. Only you can decide if the cost of a disclaimer agreement is worth the benefit of having one in your safe deposit box.

CHAPTER 8

BUSINESS PARTNERS: ENTERING AND EXITING PARTNERSHIPS

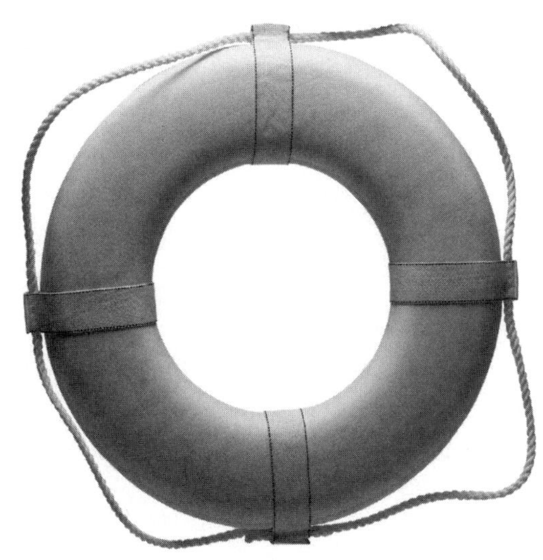

A partner is someone who works with you in your business who receives a percentage of the profits and losses of the business. While a partner may receive a "draw," or advance, against his or her share of the business profits and losses, he or she does not receive a salary as such. A partner receives a Form K-1 at the end of each year showing his or her percentage of the profits and losses of the business for that year and must pay income taxes on the amount shown on the K-1.

Partners can make contributions to the capital of the business and may be required to make additional contributions to cover cash shortfalls if your agreement so provides.

A partner can bind your company to legal agreements, even if you disagree with his or her business judgment in making the agreement. Each partner can bind all the others, even if the others don't know what the renegade partner is doing—if Partner A screws up, Partner B gets sued and could lose his house and vice versa. Lawyers call this "joint and several liability."

A partnership interest is an "asset" of his or her estate, so if a partner dies, the interest goes to the deceased partner's heirs under his or her will. The heirs become your partners, and you have to deal with them as best you can—even though they probably don't know anything about the business and may not care to work toward its future success.

Once someone becomes your business partner, the only way you can get rid of him or her (legally) is to buy them out for an agreed-upon price. You hope the partner will be reasonable in negotiating the price, but you can't be sure.

Nothing keeps you awake at night like the emotions you will feel when a business partner "goes over to the dark side," plays games with your head, or fails to hold up their end of the business.

A word here about terminology: your business "partner," as the term is used in this chapter, refers to your fellow partners in a general or limited partnership, your fellow shareholders in a closely held business corporation, or your fellow members in a limited liability company or LLC (explained following). The term "partner" doesn't necessarily imply that your business is organized as a partnership in the legal sense of that term.

Joint and Several Liability

In my opinion, it's almost malpractice for an attorney to recommend that two or more people go into business as a legal partnership when, for the same amount of money, the attorney can set up a "limited liability company" or LLC for them.

A limited liability company is basically a partnership in which the partners, or "members," enjoy limited liability for each other's mistakes, accidents, and other foul-ups. So if you and I are members of an LLC and I have an accident with the company car, you and your personal assets are safe, although I may still be personally liable to the injured person as the driver of the car.

This limitation of liability extends to breaches of contract as well. If I am a member of a LLC (even the sole member) and I sign a contract on behalf of the LLC, the aggrieved party can sue the LLC and grab onto its business assets, but my personal assets are safe as long as I signed on behalf of the LLC.

Even if you have an LLC or corporation in which the problem of "joint and several liability" is considerably reduced or even eliminated, it's a good idea also to have a "management agreement" or "voting agreement" with your business partners by which you all agree not to take any action on behalf of the business unless all of the partners are unanimous in

their view that the action should be taken. Such an agreement becomes cumbersome, however, if there are more than two or three partners in the company.

The "Accidental Partnership"

Partnerships are extremely easy to form. In most states, you are not required by law to have a written partnership agreement; you can have a "handshake" agreement with your partner. Of course, any attorney worth his or her salt will insist you have a written agreement with your business partners. Why?

Because sometimes your state's partnership law doesn't give you the result you want. Let's say you and I agree to be 80/20 partners (80 for you, 20 for me), and we seal it with a handshake. A couple of years later, I think I'm the one doing all of the work in the business, while you think you're the one doing all the work (this is a typical falling out among partners). I insist on 50 percent of the partnership. We go to court. Without a written agreement, the judge has to look to the state's partnership statute for guidance. The statute says, "In the absence of a written agreement, all partners are deemed to hold equal shares in the profits and losses of the business." The judge accordingly rules that I am entitled to 50 percent of the business, which was never a part of our initial agreement. If we had a written agreement from the outset, that agreement would have taken precedence over the state partnership statute, and you would have been able to enforce your right to an 80 percent share as we originally agreed.

Partnerships are so easy to form, in fact, that sometimes you can form one by accident. Let's say you have a small business, and I am your key supplier of parts and materials. You buy all of your parts from me, and because you are such a good customer, I sometimes "customize" my parts for your business. After a few years in business together, you launch a new product, and I agree to supply all the parts for that product in exchange for a percentage of your business profits from the venture. Do you see a partnership "creeping in through the back door" here? If something bad happens with that product, no matter whether it's your fault or mine, you and I may be going down together because to the outside world we look like partners.

Let's say you visit a law firm to have your will prepared. The sign on the door says "Jones and Smith, Attorneys at Law." You want to see Mr. Smith and are handed a business card that says "Jones and Smith, Attorneys at Law." You meet with Mr. Smith, and he prepares your will. The invoice from the law firm says "Jones and Smith, Attorneys at Law." The will is defective, and your heirs lose lots of money to federal estate and death taxes. Your estate sues both Messrs. Jones and Smith for malpractice (remember that "joint and several liability"). The attorney for Mr. Jones files a motion with the court asking for the case to be dismissed against him on the grounds that "Mr. Smith and I were never really partners; we just shared office space and some expenses. We combined our names only to make things easier on the printers and save some money. I practice business law and don't know the first thing about wills—that is Mr. Smith's specialty." Sorry—the motion will almost certainly be denied.

Why? After all, you never met Mr. Jones and didn't rely on his advice for anything. Except for his name on the door, you had no reason to believe that Mr. Jones ever actually existed. Still, your estate has the right to sue Mr. Jones because he and Mr. Smith conducted their law practice in such a way that people had reason to believe they were indeed partners. If you do business with someone in such a way that you look like partners, you will be held accountable as partners, even though you never intended to create a legal partnership.

Think about this the next time you hire a subcontractor to help you do a job for a big corporate client. If the client isn't told explicitly and in writing that you have subcontracted part

of the job out, you and your subcontractor may look like partners in the client's eyes. If the subcontractor fouls up, you may be dragged into court even though you had no knowledge of his mistake and could not have prevented it even if you did.

Letting New Partners "Earn Their Way In"

Let's say you want to offer someone (such as a family member or a valued employee) an ownership interest in your business, but they don't have any money to pay for it. They are, however, willing to work for their "sweat equity." You may want to consider an "earn-in."

Here's the scenario: you are setting up a limited liability company (LLC) with your daughter. She is enthusiastic about working with you, but she has small children, and you're not sure how much time or energy she will be able to devote to the business. Initially, she will have a 10 percent ownership interest in the LLC (you will have the remaining 90 percent), but you want to set up an incentive where at the end of each year, if your daughter is still involved in the business, she will automatically get an additional 10 percent. This would happen again each year until the two of you are 50-50 partners after four years.

Sounds simple enough, doesn't it? Yet, even a simple earn-in such as this one may create significant tax problems for both parent and daughter if it is not structured very carefully.

The first step is to determine if the earn-in will be considered an "arm's length" transaction for tax purposes. An arm's length transaction is one in which the daughter receives her 10 percent ownership interest each year for "fair market value"—the same amount the parent would have accepted from an unrelated party—in either cash, property, or services.

Since it seems the daughter is receiving her ownership interest solely for services rendered (i.e., she is not paying cash), both the LLC and her services will have to be valued (at possibly significant expense) by a "qualified appraiser," who may not necessarily be the LLC's accountant or financial adviser.

Assuming this earn-in is deemed to be an arm's length transaction, the daughter will have to report the value of her services as income on her tax return for that year and pay self-employment tax on it as well. The daughter may or may not have the cash to pay the taxes due on this "phantom income," and the parent or LLC may have to help her out with a loan or a cash advance. The LLC will get a deduction, which may be allocated to the parent as the only other member of the LLC.

If the earn-in is not an arm's-length transaction, the daughter will still be required to report as income that portion of the 10 percent ownership interest deemed to have been given her in exchange for services rendered to the LLC during each year, as determined by a qualified appraiser. If the value of the 10 percent interest exceeds the value of the daughter's services, then the excess will be considered a "gift," and the parent may have to pay federal gift tax each year at substantial rates if the excess value is greater than $11,000, the parent has made more than $1 million in taxable gifts during his or her lifetime, and certain other conditions are met. The value of the 10 percent interest, the value of the daughter's services, and the amount of taxable gift will all have to be determined at significant cost.

One possible solution is to include a provision in the LLC Operating Agreement (the LLC equivalent of a partnership agreement) that any 10 percent interest received by the daughter as part of her earn-in is an interest in future profits only, such that she will have no interest in the assets of the LLC. In that case, the daughter's interest will not be treated as income, and the LLC will not be entitled to a deduction. As the radio advertisers say, though, "certain conditions and restrictions

may apply." Earn-ins have serious and often complex tax consequences, and you should always seek an accountant's help and understand the tax tradeoffs before you consider putting in place any kind of earn-in arrangement.

However the earn-in is structured for tax purposes, if I were the parent in this situation, I would talk to my attorney about the right to buy back the daughter's LLC ownership interest at a predetermined price if the daughter quits the business. If the daughter leaves the business for any reason, she will still retain the ownership interest she earned up to that point, unless she is legally required to sell it back. Without a written "buyback" agreement, if the daughter quits the business and refuses to sell out, the parent may end up working with (actually, for) a "partner" who no longer contributes to the business, but is legally entitled to a significant percentage of the business profits.

Form 5 (see page 237) is a typical earn-in provision for an LLC Operating Agreement.

When Partners Don't Hold Up Their End

What if you have a partner and the person is lying around the office, playing video games, and taking personal telephone calls all day? You're doing all the work but sharing the profits with this bozo.

The time to plan an exit strategy for an errant partner is at the very beginning of the business relationship—when everyone's friends with everyone else and everyone's "feeling the love" and willing to do whatever it takes (or so they say) to make the business a success.

Here are some strategies for getting rid of a partner that has gone bad.

STRATEGY #1: Sign Employment or Independent Contractor Agreements

In addition to your LLC operating agreement, each partner should sign an Employment Agreement or Independent Contractor Agreement (see **Form 3**) pledging to devote "substantially all of the time and expertise" to the business. The agreement should spell out the "draw" and other compensation the partner will receive and should specify that the agreement can be terminated "under the circumstances set forth in the partnership agreement." The LLC Operating Agreement should provide that if a partner breaches his Employment Agreement or Independent Contractor Agreement with the company, the other partners may, by majority vote (not counting the breaching partner), terminate the Employment Agreement or Independent Contractor Agreement. In which case, the defaulting partner will be compelled to sell his ownership equity back to the company for book value (essentially the value he would receive if the company were dissolved and liquidated and a much lower amount than the fair market value of his interest in the company).

STRATEGY #2: Create a Buy-Sell Agreement

All of the partners should sign a Buy-Sell Agreement providing that any partner who "withdraws from active participation in the management and affairs" of the company must sell his ownership stake back to the company or to the other partners for the price set out in the agreement. This agreement should, at the very least, contain the following:

- A "death and disability" clause providing for the repurchase of the interest of a deceased or disabled business partner.

- A "voluntary transfer" clause providing that before your business partner sells out to someone else either you or the company has a "right of first refusal" to buy the withdrawing partner's interest on the same terms and conditions.
- A "retirement" clause providing for the repurchase of the interest of a retiring business partner—be sure to specify the minimum age at which retirement can take place.
- A "termination of employment" clause providing that if a partner breaches his Employment Agreement or Independent Contractor Agreement with the company, the other partners may, by majority vote (not counting the breaching partner), terminate the Employment Agreement or Independent Contractor Agreement. In which case, the defaulting partner will be compelled to sell his ownership equity back to the company for book value (essentially the value he would receive if the company were dissolved and liquidated and a much lower amount than the fair market value of his interest in the company).
- An "involuntary transfer" clause providing for a repurchase of a business partner's interest in the event of bankruptcy, divorce, or other event by which he is forcibly stripped of his interest in your company.

STRATEGY #3: The "Golden Rule" Buyout

Sometimes also called a "Russian Roulette" buyout, a "Golden Rule" buyout arrangement is used in situations where a more traditional buy-sell agreement would not be appropriate.

In a Golden Rule buyout, the parties agree that in the event they disagree to such an extent that the company effectively cannot function (a "deadlock," in legal terms), each partner can offer to buy the other out for a price determined by the offering partner. The other partner then has

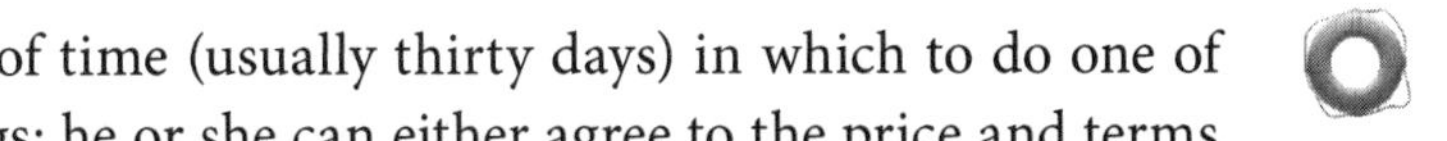

a period of time (usually thirty days) in which to do one of two things: he or she can either agree to the price and terms offered by the offering partner and sell their ownership stake, or he or she can turn around and buy the offering partner's stake in the company for the same price and terms that the offering partner proposed.

Hence the name "Golden Rule": the offering partner has the burden of making sure his or her offer is a fair one, because if it isn't, the other partner can force the offering partner to accept it himself. "Do unto others, as you would have others do unto you" is the Golden Rule, after all.

If you think about it, a Golden Rule buyout agreement is probably the fairest thing partners can agree to, since it ensures that any offer made to buy the withdrawing partner's shares is a fair one, reflecting the market value of his or her stake in the company. It is also mutual: either party can pull the trigger if they feel they are the partner better able to build the company's business going forward.

For an example of a typical Golden Rule buyout agreement, see **Form 6** in the appendix (see page 239).

Protecting Yourself If You Are a Minority Partner

Most of the protections and strategies described in this chapter are designed to protect partners who are more or less equal to their counterparts. What if you are a "minority partner," with less than 50 percent of the ownership interests in a business?

Generally, business decisions are made by a majority of the business owners (i.e., one vote more than 50 percent). In some states, two-thirds of the business owners must vote to approve certain matters, depending on the type of organization.

In any case, there are two provisions minority partners should at least attempt to negotiate in their agreements with other partners.

Supermajority voting provisions—A "supermajority voting provision" states that votes on certain key matters (such as the issuance of ownership interests to a new partner, which could decrease or "dilute" the ownership percentages of existing partners) may be made only with the approval of 100 percent (or an extremely high percentage) of the partners. This ensures that a minority partner's vote on such matters will actually have some clout. A typical supermajority voting provision appears as **Form 7** in the appendix (see page 241).

"Gross up" arrangements—In certain situations, the majority partners may take out profits from the company in such a way that minority partners incur "phantom income"—a percentage of the profits of the business that they must report as income to the IRS and pay taxes on, even though they never actually received the profits in the form of cash money.

Here's a typical example: Moe, Larry, and Curly (you always use the Three Stooges in examples like this) decide to set up a business as equal partners (one-third each). Moe and Larry are the "workers" who will run the business, while Curly is contributing money to make the business happen. Because Curly isn't sure the business will be a success, he wants to make loans to the business, which the business would then be obligated to repay with interest. That way, if the business founders, Curly will get his money out first before anyone else does.

The three partners agree that the first X dollars of profit from the business will be used to repay Curly's loans, and once those loans are paid off with interest, the three partners will share profits equally going forward.

Seems fair enough, right? Except for one thing: because Curly's loans will be coming out of the business profits, the principal portion of each loan will be treated as "profits" for tax purposes, meaning that Moe and Larry will each have to report one-third of the principal payment as income on their tax returns. If the tax due is only a few hundred dollars, it's no big deal. If the tax due is several thousand dollars, however, it is a different story.

In a situation like this what the partners should do is put a "gross up" clause into their agreement. A gross up clause obligates the company to pay any partner, upon his or her request, an amount equal to the tax due on any "phantom income" that partner may incur as a result of his or her participation in the business. That way, the affected partner will at least receive cash money to pay the taxes on their phantom income. Visit *www.cliffennico.com* to review an example of a gross up clause.

Now, you probably have noticed that the gross up payment itself will constitute income to the affected partner, which he will have to report as income on next year's tax return. Typically, gross up provisions allow for additional "grossing up" of gross up payments until the amount of the payment is less than a nominal amount, say $100.

CHAPTER 9

FAMILY AND FRIENDS: SHOULD YOU DO BUSINESS WITH THEM?

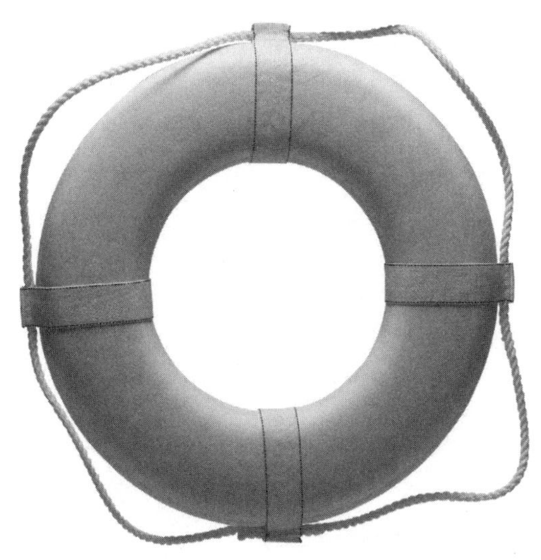

Every once in a while I see a husband and wife, brother and sister, romantic partners, or long-time friends enrolled in one of my small business seminars. When I ask them why they are thinking about starting a small business, often the answer is: "We want to be able to spend a lot more time together."

Well, you certainly won't be disappointed in that goal if you do decide to start a business. Small businesses involve long and grueling hours, and it can certainly help if you are sensitive to the other person's needs.

That sensitivity, however, has its downside as well.

When you go into business with friends or family, there are two relationships working more or less in tandem—a business relationship and a personal relationship. If you can make the two harmonize and work to your advantage, it can be a very exciting prospect indeed. Some of the most dynamic privately owned businesses in the United States today are owned by families. If the two relationships start to chafe against each other, however, life can become extremely problematic in a hurry.

Here are two pieces of advice for anyone going into business with friends and family members:

1. Don't go into business with them just because they are friends or family members—make sure they complement your strengths and weaknesses and have something to contribute to the business other than the fact that "they like you, and we get along so well together."
2. Treat them the same way you would treat a total stranger—make them sign the same paperwork and make sure you have the same protections you would obtain from a business partner who was not "friends and family."

The reasons why will become clear when we look at some examples of how mixing business and family/friendship can cause problems for a small business.

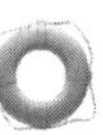

Friends and Family as Partners

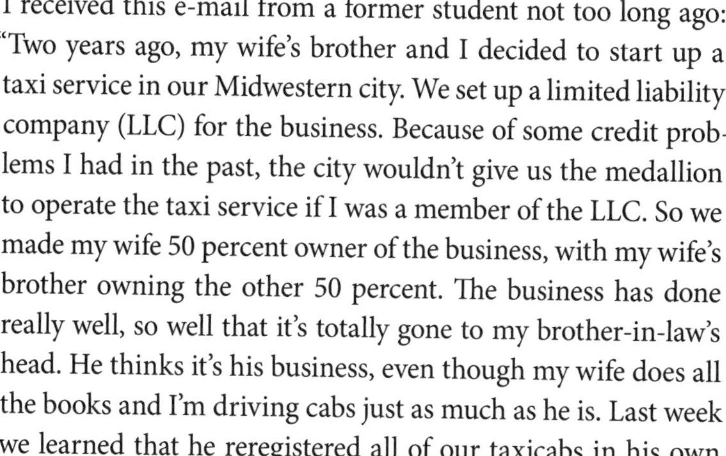

I received this e-mail from a former student not too long ago: "Two years ago, my wife's brother and I decided to start up a taxi service in our Midwestern city. We set up a limited liability company (LLC) for the business. Because of some credit problems I had in the past, the city wouldn't give us the medallion to operate the taxi service if I was a member of the LLC. So we made my wife 50 percent owner of the business, with my wife's brother owning the other 50 percent. The business has done really well, so well that it's totally gone to my brother-in-law's head. He thinks it's his business, even though my wife does all the books and I'm driving cabs just as much as he is. Last week we learned that he reregistered all of our taxicabs in his own name, shut down the LLC checking account, and opened a new LLC checking account at another bank with him as the only authorized signature. He's totally out of control. How can we get rid of him?"

There's an old saying that "the road to Hell is paved with good intentions," and here's a classic example. As noted in Chapter 8, nothing will keep a business owner awake at night as much as when a partner goes over to the dark side and starts doing weird things without your knowledge.

In this case, this person's first mistake was to set up the LLC as a 50/50 partnership between his wife and her brother. With only 50 percent of the voting power, his wife cannot legally overrule her brother's crazy behavior. She should have been given 51 percent or more of the membership interests so that her brother couldn't do any of these things without her consent.

Putting the wife in as the 50 percent member also puts her in an incredibly awkward position, emotionally speaking. She loves her husband of course, but this is her brother we're talking about. You're asking her to take sides, which cannot

be easy for her. My former student should not have assumed that she would always see things his way.

In legal terms, the wife and her brother are "deadlocked," meaning the LLC is stymied and cannot do anything because the owners can't see eye to eye. At this point, my former student and his wife have only three options: they can offer to buy her brother out; they can sue her brother (creating an even greater emotional bind); or (in most states) they can petition their state court to dissolve the LLC and divide up the assets between the wife and her brother. None of these is a really great option.

OPTION #1: Buyout

Once someone becomes your business partner, the only way you legally can get rid of him is to buy him out. When my former student set up this LLC, he should have gotten his wife's brother to sign a "buy-sell" agreement, which would have permitted his wife to buy out her brother at a preestablished price in the case of a "deadlock." The time to get an agreement like this is when everybody likes each other and nobody's thinking about getting divorced.

OPTION #2: Lawsuit

When this LLC was first set up, the wife and her brother should have signed an "Operating Agreement," similar to a partnership agreement, describing in some detail how the taxi business would be run. Now is the time for them to dig this out, dust it off, and bring it to a lawyer as fast as their feet will carry them. There's probably a provision in there that says something like "the management of the Company's business and affairs will be conducted by the Members, acting by unanimous agreement and in good faith." If there is such a provision, the wife's brother has clearly breached it by launching his own private takeover of the business, and the wife can sue him for that. Keep in mind, though, that it will probably take months, if not years, and thousands of dollars in legal fees before they get the judgment they deserve here.

Also, as my former student is now merely an employee of the LLC, there's a good chance his wife's brother will fire him if a lawsuit is filed against him.

OPTION #3: Dissolution

In many states, when an LLC is "deadlocked," an aggrieved member can ask the state courts to dissolve the LLC and divide up the assets. The trouble here is that the LLC's "medallion," or license to run a taxicab service, probably cannot be split in two. My former student will have to present a compelling case to the court and make sure that the judge awards the medallion to him and his wife, rather than to the wife's brother.

How could this situation have been avoided? Whenever a client of mine wants a 50/50 partnership with someone else, I insist that they both sign a "Golden Rule" buyout agreement (see **Form 6** in the appendix, page 239). As discussed in Chapter 8, what the agreement says is basically this: in the event of a "deadlock," either partner can make an offer to buy the other out for fair market value, as determined by the offering partner. Upon receiving the offer, the other partner has thirty days in which to do one of two things: he can either accept the offer and agree to be bought out at that price, or he can turn around and buy out the offering partner for the exact same price that was offered to him. If the other partner takes neither action within the thirty-day period, the partnership (or LLC) is dissolved, and the partner who made the offer receives 100 percent of the assets.

It's not perfect, but in a situation like this it's probably the fairest thing that can be done.

Family and Friends as Investors

There's an old saying among venture capitalists that when a new business is in the start-up phase there are only three sources of capital, known as the "three Fs"—friends, family, and fools. The idea is that a start-up business is so inherently fraught with peril that only people who love the company founders as human beings will be crazy enough to help them out with cash.

While the saying is a tad cynical, there is some truth to it. Once you've mortgaged the house, tapped the kids' education fund, and maxed out all of your credit cards, you may need additional capital to get your business off the ground, and "friends and family" (if they have deep enough pockets) may be the best (or only) place to look. Generally, friends, family, spouses, and other loved ones will be less critical of your business plan—they are investing in you, not your business. If you fall behind in paying off a loan from a family member, it is usually easier to negotiate an extension of time or a lower monthly payment—they have to be able to look you in the eye at Thanksgiving dinner, after all.

There is a downside, though, to involving your friends and family in your business plans. Some of the nastiest cases in legal history are those involving the breakups of family businesses. Family or friends who become investors may have unrealistic expectations of the role they will play in the business or may engage in emotional or irrational behavior that you will never see from a "professional" investor such as a banker or venture capitalist. Here are some examples from my files.

- John goes to his Uncle Irving and asks for money to start an antiques shop. Uncle Irving writes a check for $50,000, and John starts the business. John thinks the money was a loan from Uncle Irving. Uncle Irving, on the other hand, thinks he now owns 50 percent of the business. Except for the canceled check, there is nothing in writing to indicate whether the parties intended a loan or an investment. In five years, John's business is successful, and Irving demands his 50 percent share of profits each year since the business was founded. John's plea that the money was a "loan" from Uncle Irving falls on deaf ears.
- Mary asks her beloved Aunt Irma for $20,000 to start a greeting card business out of her home. Aunt Irma writes a check, saying, "It's a loan, Mary, but don't worry about it; you can pay it back without interest any time you like." A year later, Aunt Irma dies. Her executor, a local estate attorney, writes Mary a letter demanding immediate payment of the $20,000 loan plus interest at 18 percent per annum, claiming that the money is necessary to maximize the assets of Aunt Irma's estate. There is nothing in writing (such as a handwritten letter or a gift tax return since the gift was more than $11,000) to show Aunt Irma intended a "gift."
- Joan sells 30 percent of her fledgling Internet business to her old college roommate Rebecca for $30,000. Everything goes smoothly between the two women, and the two remain friends, until years later when, at their annual reunion over lunch, Rebecca says, "As you know, Joan, I've been having a lot of trouble with my teenage daughter Melody. She's been in and out of drug rehab clinics, is living with her rock drummer boyfriend, and has tattoos and body piercing just about everywhere you can imagine. I feel she really needs some exposure to the business

world. As a favor to me, could you find a place for Melody in your company?" When Joan refuses, Rebecca turns angry and responds, "Do you mean to tell me the business means more to you than our friendship?"

Loans Versus Investments

When a friend or family member agrees to invest in your business, they always say they are "giving you" the money. My advice is: Don't take them too literally.

There are only two ways anyone can invest in your business. Either they make a "loan" to your business, or they make an "investment" in your business in exchange for a percentage of your profits and losses. If the transaction is a "loan," the investor is entitled to repayment of the principal plus a reasonable amount of interest over a stated period of time. A loan must be paid on time, or else the lender legally has the right to demand immediate repayment of the entire loan amount and may also have the right to seize some or all of your assets and sell them at public auction to satisfy their debt. On the plus side, a "lender" has no right to manage your business, attend board meetings, or otherwise tell you what to do.

If the transaction is an investment, the investor receives a percentage of your business and is not entitled to repayment of the amount at any time. He or she gets paid whenever you have the money and are willing to do so. That's why they call investments "risk" capital. You may never get it back. The downside is that an "investor," unlike a "lender," is legally your business partner, has the right to get involved in your business, and may have the right to tell you what to do. One of the worst surprises in any small business is to wake up one morning and discover that your formerly docile partner is now legally your boss.

Whenever you take money from friends or family, you must always be clear as to whether their money is a loan or an investment. When in doubt, you should suggest your friend or family member give you a "loan" rather than an "investment." While your business will have to repay the loan on time, the friend or family member will not be your "partner" in any legal sense, and you will not have to take any of the friendly advice your investor will no doubt gratuitously offer at family get-togethers! Besides, if your business takes off and the friend or family member gets a wee bit too nosy, you can always pay off the loan with interest and put them in your rearview mirror.

Get It on Paper

Whether you structure your relationship with a friend or family member as a loan or an investment, you should always make sure to prepare and sign the same legal paperwork you would require if the investor was a total stranger. One of the biggest mistakes business owners make when dealing with friends and family members is to make deals with a handshake, assuming that the friendship or family relationship will continue the way it always has.

There is an old Chinese proverb that says, "success has a thousand fathers, but failure is an orphan." Once you've taken money from a friend or family member, fights won't happen as long as your business is struggling and not showing a profit. Why? Because they are friends or family who will always support you, win or lose? No. Fights usually don't happen at this stage because there is nothing to fight over. If your investors ever want to see their money back with some kind of return, they have a natural inclination to be patient, cooperate with you, and help you out whenever they can.

Once your business takes off like a bottle rocket, however, fights are more likely to break out because the stakes have now suddenly become much higher. The individual who said he would "loan" you some money to help you get started now remembers you said something about giving him or her 20 percent of your company (as in my first example with Uncle Irving).

Sometimes your friend or family member dies (as in my second example with Aunt Irma). Before, you were dealing with a sweet, loving benefactor. Today, you are dealing with a gimlet-eyed estate attorney (or worse yet, a greedy heir) whose sole priority is to get as much money as possible out of your business. Perhaps your investor has had a change in lifestyle—marriage, divorce, a battle with cancer, a new boyfriend or girlfriend who thinks they know all about business—that causes them to look at the world differently than they did before.

One of the biggest mistakes people make when dealing with friends or family members is to assume that they will always be the same as they are today. Thankfully, I am not the same person today that I was in my twenties or even my thirties. Some of the people who were my closest friends back then are strangers to me now. Some of the people with whom I wanted nothing to do back then are today my closest friends.

If there is no legal paperwork with the friend or family member to indicate what your intentions were when the investment was made, it is entirely "your word against theirs," and you probably will have to give them something to which they were never entitled to keep them from suing you or creating embarrassment within your family or circle of friends.

If the transaction is a "loan," your business should draft a Promissory Note, a corporate IOU that sets out the amount borrowed, the rate of interest, and the repayment period.

When dealing with friends or family members, consider a "cash flow" Promissory Note in which your business promises to repay the loan "as and when it is capable of doing so" without a fixed repayment schedule. Visit www.cliffennico.com for a "Cash Flow" Promissory Note. If the loan is to be collateralized or "secured" by your business assets, additional documents (such as a Security Agreement and a UCC-1 Financing Statement) will have to be prepared and filed with state and local government agencies.

If the transaction is an "investment," your business and the investor should sign a Subscription Agreement, which sets out the amount of the investment, the percentage ownership you are giving up in exchange for the investment, and the investors' rights and limitations as a part owner of your company. A Subscription Agreement can also be found at www.cliffennico.com.

Documents relating to loans and investments can become quite complicated and should always be prepared by an attorney who specializes in commercial or business law.

Your Investor Is Your Partner

One of the great myths of owning your own business is that there actually are human beings in the world who will contribute money to your business and then stay out of your hair and let you run it without breathing down your neck every ten minutes. In my experience, investing in a friend's or relative's business is a traumatic experience for most people, and sooner or later they will become neurotic about getting their money back.

Friends and family members who become investors may start acting just like business partners, whether they are legally entitled to or not. You will need to treat them with "kid gloves" because they are, after all, friends and family members, and

you will have to face them when birthdays, anniversaries, and the holidays roll around.

Friends and family members may feel a certain "entitlement" to ask for favors and make demands upon you and your business, whether they are legally entitled to or not (as in my third example involving Rebecca and her wayward teenage daughter).

Friends and family members may think they have become "instant experts" in your business by virtue of their investment, offering well-meaning but gratuitous (and sometimes downright stupid) advice. Because they are after all your friends and family members, you cannot simply ignore them.

Business versus Friendship

Finally, always keep in mind that whenever friends and family members become investors there are two relationships going on—a business relationship and a personal relationship, and sometimes the two come into conflict. To do what is right for your business (for example, taking money from a new investor that decreases your family's or friend's percentage ownership of the business) may risk jeopardizing the personal relationship. Similarly, to do what is right for your personal relationship (for example, giving in to your investor's request that an unsuitable relative be given a job in your company) may risk jeopardizing the success of your business. Whenever a friend or family member invests in your business, you should be prepared to spend a considerable amount of time "holding their hands," monitoring their ever-changing moods and circumstances, and keeping them informed of your business progress and problems to avoid the nightmare of having to choose between a successful business and a happy relationship.

Friends and Family as Employees: When Business Separates Father and Son

Here's an e-mail that will really tug at your heart—it did mine.

> *I am a seventy-five-year-old former engineer. Thirty years ago I founded a small consumer goods company that today has over $2 million in sales. I sit on the Board of Directors with my only son, who has been with me in the business for over 10 years, and the company accountant. I own 70 percent of the company's stock, and my son owns 20 percent.*
>
> *The company last made a profit three years ago. At that time my son started a sideline business—a commercial real estate firm—that purchased the building my company currently occupies. My son then arranged the transfer of the company to this building at a bargain rent and began investing in additional facilities and personnel as part of his plan to grow the company.*
>
> *We soon ran out of money, and my son asked me to give him my President and CEO title to help his search for additional funding. Over $3 million of new funding has come from my son's real estate company in the form of loans collateralized by the company's assets.*
>
> *My son has become increasingly committed to his real estate business, and I can't blame him because he has really prospered there. Unfortunately, he is spending very little time in managing my company's business. He only comes into the office one day a week and has appointed a golfing buddy of his as General Manager. I see no change in the company's position since this person took over a year and half ago.*

I started the company using my own resources and later brought in my son to manage the business, help it grow, and eventually become my successor. My goal was to build a successful business that would provide a comfortable retirement for my wife and me and to provide a comfortable life for my three children. That hasn't happened, and I'm afraid we are running out of time.

I intend to fire my son and take over as CEO while I search for a new one to replace my son and turn this business around. What is the best way to do this?

To start with, Father has only one seat out of three on the Board of Directors and so will not be able to oust Son directly without getting the third Director—the company accountant—on board. The company accountant (if he or she has any sense) probably will resign from the Board rather than be put in the position of "arbitrating" between Father and Son—a position that might create a "conflict of interest" for the accountant, who presumably has been taking his marching orders from the Son or the General Manager.

But with 70 percent of the stock, Father should be able to call a special meeting of the company's stockholders (both the Son and the owners of the 10 percent of company stock not owned by Father and Son will have to receive written notice and an opportunity to attend the meeting) and elect a new Board of Directors consisting of just himself. Once that is accomplished, as the sole Director of the company, Father can hire and fire anyone he pleases, including Son and his friend the General Manager.

Before Father pulls that trigger, it's important to know which way the gun is pointed. The son, through his real estate firm, has made $3 million in loans to the company, presumably to meet payroll and other operating expenses (since the "disinterested" members of a company's Board of Directors must vote on shareholder loans, Father and the company accountant probably approved them). These loans are collateralized by the company's assets. It's very likely that these are "demand" loans that the Son, or his real estate firm, can call at any time if Son is unhappy with the way things are going at the company. By ousting Son from his CEO job, Father almost certainly will get the Son really mad—after all, the Son may honestly feel that he has been "doing his Dad a favor" by keeping the company on "life support" out of his own pocket (let's not forget the bargain rent for the office space) with little prospect of a return—so mad that he may call in the loans. With only $2 million a year in sales and zero profits, the company will not be able to repay these loans on demand, and Son will end up foreclosing on the company's assets, leaving Father (and indeed all stockholders) with empty hands and worthless stock.

If I were the Father in this situation, I would call a meeting of the Board of Directors for the stated purpose of "discussing the company's future and any ownership or management changes that may be necessary to ensure the company's future profitability." That should send a signal to the Son (if he doesn't already suspect) that Father is unhappy and creates an opportunity for Father and Son to discuss the situation calmly and intelligently, without finger-pointing. By treating the company's situation as a business problem and not a family dispute, there is a chance the company accountant, who as a Director has some legal and ethical responsibility to act in the company's best interests without "taking sides," may be more willing to offer constructive suggestions and compromises that will resolve the impasse between Father and Son. This is not a perfect solution, but it's probably the best one possible given how badly the situation at this company has already deteriorated.

At the age of seventy-five, the Father probably views this business as his "life's work" or "legacy" and so has an emotional investment in the company that goes far beyond the labor and money he put into it over the years. It is very possible that this company may fail despite everyone's best efforts. The fact that the company needs the Son's personal loans to meet operating expenses hints at problems that go far beyond his "absentee management," and Father and Son both need to confront these directly and honestly. It may be that Father and Son should both accept the inevitable and shut down the company (or sell it) to limit their future losses and preserve their relationship. Perhaps there's a cushy job opening for Father at that very successful real estate firm Son is running.

Keeping Your Neighbors at Bay (If You Have a Home Office)

Once you've experienced the freedom of working from home, it's hard to imagine ever going back to an office, a cubicle, or a storefront. When you are an advocate of home-based business, as I am, you are tempted to believe that just about any business can be run from home.

Yet, there are some businesses that cannot (and should not!) be run from a home office. Let's consider some examples.

EXAMPLE #1: Businesses That Are Noisy or Smelly

If your business is one that will generate lots of noise or noxious odors on a regular basis, you absolutely should not run it out of your home. While zoning laws in many communities have been relaxed to accommodate home-based businesses, any business that changes the character of your neighborhood (i.e., makes it look and sound like a commercial or industrial district) will still face a zoning challenge, especially if the neighbors complain. Your neighbors may also be able to sue you for "nuisance," which is a form of trespass on their property rights. So if you are planning to start a meatpacking business, find an abandoned warehouse or factory space. Do not practice your trade in the basement.

EXAMPLE #2: Businesses That Generate Lots of Traffic or Are Highly Visible

Similarly, if you are going to have customers or clients visiting you at all hours of the day and night or more than one or two employees working with you, you are best advised not to conduct business out of your home. If the local children can't ride their bikes or play softball in the street after school because there are too many cars parked in the street outside your home or if they will be too busy dodging UPS or FedEx trucks making their hourly deliveries to your home office, it is only a matter of time before your neighbors will complain to the local authorities about your business activities.

EXAMPLE #3: Businesses That Must Comply with Health and Safety Laws

Like many people, you have wondered if it is possible to run a small-time catering or specialty food business out of your home. Generally, the answer is "no." In most states, commercial food establishments must operate a "legal kitchen" conforming to state (and sometimes also municipal) health and safety regulations, and few home kitchens have the equipment, ventilation, and other amenities that these regulations will require.

Beyond keeping your kitchen spotlessly clean, for example, you may be required to:

- Use a compartmentalized sink with a grease trap installed, with a separate sink for washing hands
- Use covered lights, with clear plastic tubes that cover the fluorescent bulbs
- Use nonabsorbent material for washable surfaces such as walls, floors, cabinets, countertops, and ceilings
- Separate your refrigerator, freezer, and oven by specified distances
- Have a separate entrance to the kitchen and a heating and air-conditioning system separate from that of the house generally
- Bar pets and nonemployees from the kitchen area
- Maintain a "handicapped access" bathroom for your employees (even if you are the only employee and you are not handicapped)

Even if you comply with these regulations, you will have to maintain certain records and submit to periodic health and safety inspections, frequently without notice, which may disrupt your family life and routine.

As a general rule, if working out of rented commercial or industrial space will lower your cost of complying with government regulations (because presumably the landlord has already done some of the work for you), you should do so.

EXAMPLE #4: Businesses That Must Have an "Established" Look

Finally, there are some businesses that customers and clients just won't take seriously if operated from a home office.

When I am asked if it is possible to run a law practice from a home office, for example, my response is always, "It depends upon the type of practice." In my law practice, I represent only small businesses and self-employed professionals.

Many of these folks work from home themselves and like the fact that I operate as informally as they do. They don't mind meeting me in diners, rented offices, or parking lots when documents need to be signed. They appreciate the fact that because my overhead is extremely low, I can charge "rock bottom" prices for the more basic legal services. As one of my clients put it awhile back, "If I walk into a law office and see lots of expensive paintings and furniture, I know darn well who's paying for it." Having a home office actually gives me a competitive advantage in attracting start-up businesses as clients.

But let's consider another type of law practice. Let's say I was a "trusts and estates" lawyer, and you wanted me to draft your will. This is a very personal, emotional decision on your part—not only are you confronting your own mortality (a stressful thing for most of us), but you are entrusting me with the financial well-being of your entire family. It is, frankly, one of the most important things you will do in life, and you want to be extremely confident in the person doing the legal work.

If you are like most people, you will want to know that the lawyer drafting your will is established, successful, and has done this thing a thousand times before. You want to work with a lawyer, or a firm, that looks as if he or it has been around for a hundred years. You want to see an oak-paneled office, with perhaps Currier & Ives prints on the wall, plush leather furniture, and lots of bookcases full of well-thumbed legal volumes. Instead, I am giving you directions to my home office. You find yourself driving through a residential neighborhood and stopping at a ranch-style house with a swing set in the backyard. I greet you wearing a T-shirt, Bermuda shorts, sunglasses, and a baseball cap because I have just been playing Frisbee with my dog. I break out my legal pad and start asking intimate questions about your family tree while we are sitting around the kitchen table and my dog is bugging me to continue the Frisbee game that was so rudely interrupted.

Even if I've got the best reputation in town for drafting wills, how comfortable do you feel? If you are like most folks, you probably will be a little nervous. Discussing your will with your attorney is something that can only be done in a certain atmosphere, and my home office setup simply does not create that atmosphere.

If you sense that your customers or clients will be more comfortable by your projecting an "established" image, then you probably should rent office space for your business (and hire a good interior designer to decorate it—one who has designed offices for other similar businesses in the area).

CHAPTER 10

HEIRS, SUCCESSORS, AND OLD AGE

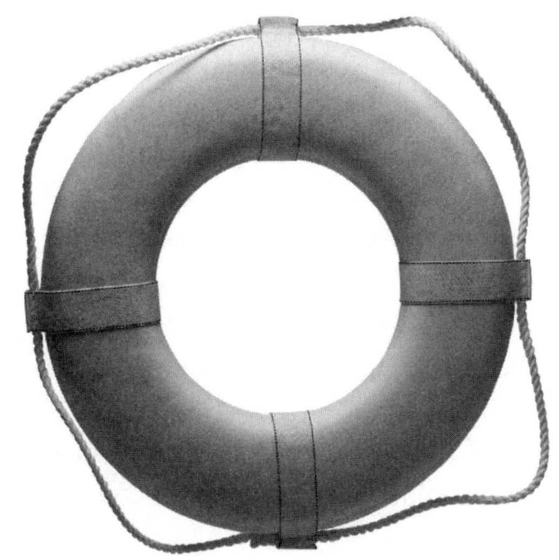

At my college graduation almost thirty years ago, one of several family members in attendance was my beloved Aunt Mary. Aunt Mary was what you might call a "lovable curmudgeon"—she smoked about three packs of cigarettes a day, drank two martinis with lunch, and refused to vote in the 1964 presidential election because she thought both Lyndon Johnson and Barry Goldwater were "too soft on the Communists." Get the picture?

Well, my graduating class was a pretty scruffy lot—long hair and beards, faded jeans, sneakers and ties tied in sixty different directions, and a few brave souls smoking controlled substances in the back row. I admit that during the ceremony, I couldn't wait to get Aunt Mary's opinion on the future leaders of the United States.

So as soon as I had rejoined my family, diploma in hand, and managed to get Aunt Mary alone (she had promised my parents to be on her best behavior that weekend), I asked her, "So, Aunt Mary, what do you think of today's college generation?" I fully expected her to explode in righteous indignation about the decline of Western civilization and the decay of morals.

What she said came as a total surprise, and I will never forget it as long as I live. She merely shook her head and said, sadly, "You know, Cliff, I really feel sorry for you young people nowadays. You don't realize it, and this won't make sense right now, but believe me someday it will . . . you young people today are going to make terrible old people."

You had to know Aunt Mary to understand what she was saying. She wasn't just knocking or "dissing" the Baby Boomer generation out of hand. She was, in fact, saying something rather profound.

If she had the education to speak her mind clearly, I think it would have come out something like this: "You young people have had it relatively easy in your lives. Our generation had the Great Depression, World War II, and the Cold War to deal with. We not only survived it, but also we defeated everything that life could throw up against us. Your generation hasn't been challenged like that. You've known nothing but peace and prosperity, and you will have trouble dealing with adversity only because you're not accustomed to it. When you get older, you inevitably have to make tradeoffs and compromises with life, and your generation will have trouble dealing with that. You will do everything you can to deny, avoid, and fight against your increasingly limited ability to do things and by so doing will end up either extremely frustrated, extremely ridiculous, or both."

I sincerely hope my Aunt Mary was wrong about us; I really do. But I also have to hand her some debating points. "Letting go" of our youth, our achievements, our businesses, and our careers will be more difficult for us than it was for previous generations. Developing a strategy for that transition and planning our business so that it will survive us is the subject of this chapter.

Planning for Your Golden Years Now

Let's face it, we are all growing older. Those of us who started our home-based businesses in our midlife years (35 to 55) are looking at the prospect of retiring within the next twenty years. That is, of course, if we retire at all!

Whatever your age or the nature of your business, now is the time to begin planning for your "golden years." The good news is that, thanks to recent tax law changes, self-employed people have more options than ever before to save for retirement. The bad news is that you will not be able to count on Social Security to be there when you will need it the most. Unlike the "Greatest Generation" that has already retired, the

Baby Boom generation will be pretty much on its own when it comes to financial support during the retirement years. What about later generations? Fuhgeddaboudit—they will be too busy taking care of us!

First of all, you need insurance. Even in the smallest business, you should have:

- Life insurance in an amount sufficient to at least pay off all your business debts should you die unexpectedly
- Disability insurance (remember my broken foot from Chapter 1?)
- Long-term care insurance (be sure to buy this before you reach age fifty, otherwise the premiums may skyrocket out of reach)

Next, you need a retirement plan. There is no specific retirement planning strategy that is best for people with their own small businesses. The plan you will select will be the one that (1) sets aside the maximum amount of money tax-free for your retirement and (2) gives you the biggest tax breaks on your federal and state tax returns each year.

Each type of plan comes with its own set of rules. One basic thing to remember is that if you have employees, you must be cautious when implementing a plan. You need to know what the impact will be on your employees. You may be happy to see what you can "sock away" for yourself, but may not be as happy when you realize how much you have to "sock away" for your employees.

Assuming that most home-based businesses involve only one proprietor (that's you), with perhaps one or two part-time employees (any larger than that and you should seriously reconsider working out of the home), here are some things you should discuss with your financial and tax advisors:

- Traditional or Roth IRAs
- Simplified Employee Pensions, or SEP-IRAs
- Savings Incentive Match Plan for Employees (SIMPLEs)
- Keogh Plans
- 401(k) and profit-sharing plans

Keeping Management "All in the Family"

Suppose you want to leave your business to a number of relatives, but you really want your son Joe to be in charge of running the business? There are a number of ways to make sure that happens, but the most effective is for all of the owners of your business (including you) to include a "management provision" in your partnership agreement, operating agreement (for an LLC), or shareholders' agreement (for a closely held corporation). This provision would effectively say "as long as I am an owner/partner/member/shareholder of the Company, I will vote for Joe to be the President of the Company."

That way, when you die, all of your heirs who receive an ownership stake in your business are bound by the agreement and must continue to keep Joe in the President's chair. **Form 8** in the appendix (see page 242) is a typical "management and control" clause for a Buy-Sell Agreement (see Chapter 8 for more on buy-sell agreements).

Planning Your Estate

We all know to leave our estate to our spouses in our wills because transfers between spouses are exempt from federal and state death taxes. But here's a question most of us don't like to face: What if you and your spouse were to die together

in a plane crash? Who would get your assets, specifically the ownership interest in your business?

You could leave the business to a child, a family member who has worked in the business and will be able to keep it going, or to a key employee who has served you long and faithfully in the business. All are nice gestures, but your estate will be clobbered with taxes, especially if the currently planned phaseout of the federal estate tax is not made permanent between now and 2010. We have all heard stories about family-owned businesses that have had to be sold or liquidated just to pay the estate taxes.

Sooner or later, you have to accept the fact that someday there will be a world without you in it, and if you don't plan for that day, you risk losing everything you have worked your entire life to achieve. In my town there is a two-acre parcel of land with an old dilapidated building (the local "haunted house" for at least one generation of kids) on it that has been abandoned for over twenty years. There is nothing exceptional about that until you realize one thing: It's in a prime commercial location right off the exit ramp of an interstate highway. Everyone who has taken this exit or has gone on the entrance ramp back onto the interstate for the past twenty years has had to pass this derelict property. What's wrong with this picture? Why hasn't someone come along and developed this absolutely perfect location for a restaurant, fast-food outlet, or retail store?

Back in the 1970s, the property had indeed been home to a highly successful fast-food outlet owned by a man with several children and several siblings who each had several children. Due to poor estate planning, when the owner died the property was divided between twenty-three different relatives, who immediately started suing each other over who was going to run the business. The few employees who had run the fast-food outlet quit in frustration because they weren't receiving their paychecks, and the fast-food franchiser, being in dire financial straits (eventually filing for bankruptcy), was in no position to step in and take over the outlet. The store closed in 1981, and the property has been abandoned ever since. The old fast-food sign overlooking the interstate, rusting away, was a local landmark until the early 1990s, when it blew down in a storm.

Every once in awhile, a developer tries to buy the property and do right by it but becomes frustrated when he realizes he has to deal separately with the twenty-three heirs (some of whom have since died and passed their share of the nightmare among several of their own heirs, further complicating matters), their attorneys, and their interminable lawsuits, which continue to tie up the local courts to this day. I honestly think it would be easier to sell a nuclear waste dump than this property, and it will probably be decades before anyone will make money from it again.

Make no mistake—poor estate planning can kill a small business.

There are a number of strategies business owners can adopt to ensure a smooth and relatively tax-advantaged transfer of their equity to children and other heirs. Basically, these strategies fall into two broad categories: "outright" transfers during a business owner's life, and "testamentary" transfers, which only occur upon the business owner's death.

All of the techniques discussed in this chapter are relatively complex; because you are exploiting loopholes in the Tax Code, the IRS insists that you strictly follow the rules or else they will blow apart your planning strategy and subject the value of your entire business ownership interest to the estate tax. Accordingly, none of these techniques should be undertaken without the assistance of an attorney in your area who specializes in both estate and tax matters.

Gifts During Your Lifetime

The first category of strategies you can employ to transfer your business assets involves making gifts during your lifetime.

Lifetime Gifts

The IRS allows you to make outright gifts of up to $11,000 worth of your equity each year to anyone you like. By doing so, of course, the people you give stock to become your legal partners in the business. If you own a corporation or limited liability company (LLC), you may be able to restrict their ability to become involved in the management of your business (until, of course, you're ready for them to do so) by creating two classes of stock or LLC membership interest—one having voting rights and the other having nonvoting rights—and giving your heirs only the nonvoting shares or membership interests. That way, your heirs get an economic piece of the pie but have no legal right to second-guess your management decisions.

In making outright gifts to children or other relatives, you should be sure that the transfer won't be treated as a taxable gift for income tax purposes. Otherwise they will incur "phantom income" (see Chapter 8), and they won't be too happy about that.

Family Limited Partnerships

Family limited partnerships (FLPs) are discussed at length in Chapter 6. Basically, you set up a limited partnership (or, increasingly, a limited liability company or LLC) with yourself as general partner and your heirs as limited partners, transfer all of the equity in your business to the limited partnership, and gradually decrease your ownership equity for a period of years while simultaneously increasing your heirs' equity in the business. These are extremely tricky from a tax perspective, and some recent cases in the federal courts have cast a shadow on precisely how FLPs should be set up to avoid adverse tax consequences to you and your heirs. Do not try to put a FLP together without the assistance of a capable tax and estate lawyer, since you are courting disaster if you do so.

Transfers upon Your Death

The second category of strategies involves those things you can decide on now that will come into play after your death.

"Key Person" Life Insurance

If you are young enough and can afford the premiums, you should consider taking out a "key person" life insurance policy on yourself, naming your company as beneficiary. That way, upon your death, the company will receive the insurance proceeds (tax-free), which can then be used to pay federal and estate death taxes without impacting the cash flow from your business. A provision for a buy-sell agreement requiring a company to pay the premiums on a policy of "key person life insurance" is available at www.cliffennico.com.

Buy-Sell Agreement with Life Insurance

This strategy only works if the person you want to take over your business upon your death is already a part owner of the business. Basically, you would enter a buy-sell agreement with your successor (see Chapter 8) providing that upon the death of either the other must buy out the deceased owner's estate for a specified amount. Then, each owner takes out a policy of life insurance on the other, naming himself as

beneficiary. For example, Owner A would take out a life insurance policy on Owner B, naming Owner A as beneficiary. That way, upon Owner B's death, Owner A would cash in on the policy and use that to repurchase Owner B's interest from his estate, pay estate and death taxes, and so forth. The problem is that if Owner B is of an advanced age, the premiums for even basic life insurance coverage can be extremely expensive because of the actuarial probability of death during the early years of the policy. The buy-sell agreement should specifically require Owner A to use the life insurance proceeds to repurchase Owner B's interest and for no other purpose; otherwise, Owner A may be tempted to bag the business and head for Vegas.

One more thing to think about: maybe I've been watching too many episodes of *The Sopranos*, but I'm not sure I would want my business partner to have a policy on my life for more than I'm worth.

Credit Shelter Trust

A credit shelter trust is a tax-planning trust that assures that your federal estate tax exemption is "sheltered" rather than wasted by your death. It can be established during your lifetime or upon death, depending on whether you want to avoid probate or not. It allows you and your spouse to pass on an estate worth up to $1,000,000 without incurring federal or state death taxes.

Here's how it works. The government allows individuals to pass on an estate worth up to $1,000,000 without incurring estate or gift taxes. However, spouses are exempt from this rule and have the ability to give an unlimited amount to each other during life or at death. This unique exemption from estate and gift taxes is called the "marital deduction," and much planning is done to avoid its traps.

Let's say that your combined estate is worth $2,000,000, and you have a will leaving everything to your spouse. If you die first, your estate will not incur any transfer taxes since the marital deduction allows you to pass on an unlimited amount to your spouse. However, if your spouse dies at the same time you do, your spouse's estate will pay $435,000 in federal estate tax since he or she can only give away $1,000,000 and no longer has a marital deduction because of your death.

If instead you had given $1,000,000 to a credit shelter trust for the benefit of your spouse, children, or other beneficiaries, you would have fully used your exemption amount ($1,000,000) by giving it to some entity other than your spouse. The remaining $1,000,000 could have been given to your spouse, and since your spouse also has the ability to give up to $1,000,000 to anyone without incurring estate tax, no estate tax is due on your spouse's death.

Be careful—by putting your entire estate into a credit shelter trust, you may not be leaving your spouse enough to live on!

Generation-Skipping Trusts and Dynasty Trusts

IRS rules and state laws that prohibited the creation of trusts "in perpetuity" (meaning forever) are gradually being relaxed to allow "dynasty trusts" in which people can leave assets directly to their grandchildren or great-grandchildren (a "generation-skipping trust") or in trust for many future generations (a "dynasty trust"). By leaving minority interests in your business to your heirs, you may be exempt from federal "generation-skipping taxes" on such arrangements. Talk to a tax lawyer to find out if your state currently allows these. The law is in a state of flux right now, and you still can't create these in some states because of something called the "Rule Against Perpetuities" that has been around since the Middle Ages.

CHAPTER 11

LAWYERS, ACCOUNTANTS, AND OTHER PROFESSIONALS: HOW THEY CAN STEAL YOUR SUCCESS

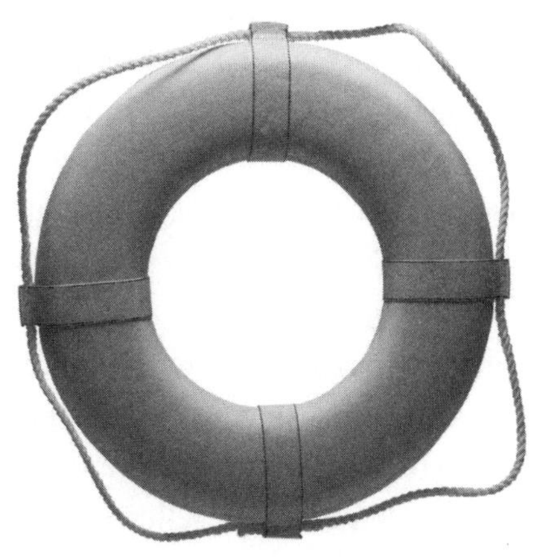

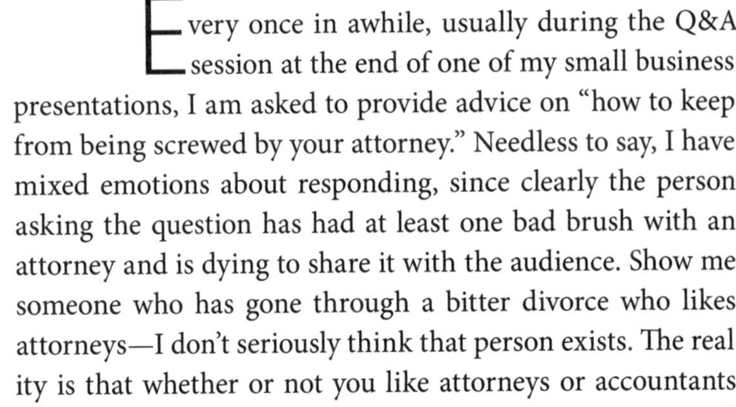

Every once in awhile, usually during the Q&A session at the end of one of my small business presentations, I am asked to provide advice on "how to keep from being screwed by your attorney." Needless to say, I have mixed emotions about responding, since clearly the person asking the question has had at least one bad brush with an attorney and is dying to share it with the audience. Show me someone who has gone through a bitter divorce who likes attorneys—I don't seriously think that person exists. The reality is that whether or not you like attorneys or accountants really doesn't matter; if you plan to build a business, you will have to develop a strong professional relationship with members of both professions if you plan to succeed.

But the question is a valid one, not just because there are a lot of unscrupulous professionals out there (maybe there are, maybe there aren't), but also because a lot of miscommunications occur between business owners and professional advisors (even the most ethical and well-intentioned ones) that can cause problems for the business.

I once knew an attorney who was the absolute "poster child" for ethical behavior in his profession; he made it a point of going out of his way to "do the right thing" at all times, even if he had to eat a portion of his fee. Awhile ago, this attorney represented a young person in the purchase of a small business—a hardware store. The client had worked several years as an employee in the store, and the seller, not having any children, wanted this young person to take over the business. My attorney friend put together an absolutely perfect deal that was fair to both parties and protected everyone, although it involved the young buyer paying off the purchase price in installments over several years. However, could be no assurance the store could generate enough revenue for the buyer to both pay the store's operating expenses and make his payments to the seller in timely fashion (in addition to the buyer's family). The buyer wasn't discouraged since he had plans to build the business and increase revenue and felt that "stretching a bit" to accommodate the seller's needs would give him the incentive he needed to grow the business beyond its current level.

At a party shortly after the closing of this transaction, my attorney friend encountered an executive who had just recently been downsized from a major corporation. The executive, hearing of my friend's specialty in representing small businesses, told my friend he had a huge severance package that he wanted to invest in small businesses, adding "I don't really want to run a business myself, but if you know someone with a strong business who can use a partner with years of experience and a huge Rolodex of contacts, please let me know." My friend immediately thought of the struggling young hardware store owner and thought he should introduce him to the executive, reasoning that if the executive invested a huge amount of cash into the business that the young store owner could pay off the seller's note right away and devote all of the business revenue to paying expenses.

The attorney spoke to the young store owner and gave him the executive's card, explaining what the executive was looking for, assuring the young store owner of the executive's good intentions, and saying very clearly that he (the attorney) had no vested interest in the matter—he "just thought it wouldn't hurt for the two of you to have lunch and see if you like each other."

Shortly thereafter, my client got a telephone call from a friend of the young store owner, who was also a client. The friend said, "I just thought you'd want to know that our friend Joe over at the hardware store is extremely upset with you—he's badmouthing you all over town." My attorney friend was deeply hurt and surprised and asked why. The friend responded, "Well, he's saying that only a couple of

weeks after you closed his deal with the former owner, you approached him and told him you 'knew this guy with a lot of money' who could become his business partner and that he should seriously consider it. Joe couldn't understand why you would do such a thing after spending so much time and effort making sure Joe would be the one to own the business 100 percent, without any need for a partner. He just figures that you don't believe he has what it takes to build this business and that you have some kind of ulterior motive in doing this. I told him you were a good guy and all, but he's really ticked off at you. He told me some relatives of his had warned him 'Watch out, you know about attorneys, sooner or later they all try to screw you.'"

Needless to say, Joe the young store owner was not very sophisticated in the ways of business and was very ill-advised by his relatives. Given his relationship with my attorney friend and my friend's unblemished record and reputation as an extremely ethical attorney, Joe should have given him the benefit of the doubt. But these things happen in lawyer-client relationships every once in awhile; what my attorney friend learned from this experience is the meaning of the classic phrase "no good deed ever goes unpunished."

How can professionals steal your success? Basically, in one of three ways:

- The professional takes on work that he's unable to do because he's unfamiliar with the area of law involved or has never before done the particular type of transaction.
- The professional charges too much for the work he does.
- The professional is not adept at managing his time and juggling multiple clients. As a result, the client's urgent telephone calls are ignored, and important deadlines are missed.

Finding the Right Lawyer or Accountant for Your Business

There are two professionals every business will need early on: an accountant and a lawyer. The reasons for hiring an accountant are pretty obvious—you need someone to help you set up your "chart of accounts," review your numbers periodically, and prepare all of your necessary federal, state, and local tax returns. The reason for hiring a business attorney may not, however, be so apparent. A good business attorney will provide vital assistance in almost every aspect of your business, from basic zoning compliance to copyright and trademark advice, from drafting contracts to formal business incorporation, and from employment law issues to figuring out whether a business expense is tax-deductible. You get the idea.

First, here are some general rules about dealing with lawyers.

RULE #1: If You Are Being Sued, It's Too Late

Most small businesses put off hiring a lawyer until the sheriff is standing at the door serving them with a summons. This is a bad mistake. The time to hook up with a good business lawyer is before you are sued. Once you have been served with a summons and complaint, it's too late. The problem has already occurred, and it's just a question of how much you will have to pay (in court costs, attorneys' fees, settlements, and other expenses) to get the problem resolved. The U.S. judicial system is a lot like a Roach Motel—it's easy to get into court, but very difficult to get out once you've been "trapped." Most lawyers agree that nobody likes to pay attorneys' fees for anything, but the fee a lawyer will charge to keep you out of trouble is only a small fraction of the fee a lawyer will charge to get you out of trouble once it's happened.

RULE #2: Decide If a Big Firm or Small Firm Is Best for You

Generally speaking, the larger the law firm, the greater the overhead, therefore the higher the hourly rates you will be expected to pay. Still, larger firms have a number of advantages over smaller ones. Over the past twenty years, lawyers have become incredibly specialized. If you use a solo practitioner or small firm as your lawyer(s), it's likely that they will not have all the skills you may need to grow business. I don't know of any solo practitioner and very few small firms (fewer than ten lawyers) that could handle your lawsuits, negotiate your lease of office or retail space, file a patent or trademark, draft a software license agreement, advise you on terminating a disruptive employee, and oversee your corporate annual meeting. Sooner or later, these "generalists" will have to refer you out to specialists, and you will find yourself dealing with two or three (or even more) attorneys.

While larger firms are more expensive to deal with, they have two significant advantages: (1) they usually have all the legal skills you need "under one roof" and (2) they have a lot of clout in the local, regional, and (perhaps) national legal community. A nasty letter from a "powerhouse" law firm with offices in thirty states is a lot more intimidating than a nasty letter from a solo practitioner who is not admitted to practice in the defendant's state. Also, being connected with a large, well-established law firm may have intangible benefits—they may be willing to introduce you to financing sources or let you use their name as a reference when seeking partnership arrangements. Certainly if you run a fast-growing entrepreneurial company that plans to go public (or sell out to a big company) someday, you would need to work with lawyers whose names are recognized in the investment banking and venture capital communities.

What Kind of Lawyer Should You Choose?

Like doctors, lawyers are becoming increasingly specialized. Someone who does mostly wills, house closings, and other "nonbusiness" matters is probably not a good fit for your business. At the very least, you will need the following sets of skills. The more skills that reside in the same human being, the better!

Contracts—You will need a lawyer who can understand your business quickly, prepare the standard form contracts you will need with customers, clients, and suppliers, and help you respond to contracts that other people will want you to sign.

Business organizations—You will need a lawyer who can help you decide whether a corporation or limited liability company (LLC) is the better way to organize your business and can prepare the necessary paperwork.

Taxes and licenses—Although your accountant will prepare and file your business tax returns each year, your lawyer should know how to register your business for federal and state tax identification numbers and understand the tax consequences of the more basic business transactions in which your business will engage.

Intellectual property—If you are in a media, design, or other "creative" type business, it is certainly a plus if your lawyer can help you register your products and services for federal trademark and copyright protection. Generally, these tasks are performed by specialists who do nothing but intellectual property legal work. If your lawyer says he or she "specializes in small businesses," then he or she should have a close working relationship with one or more intellectual property specialists.

Tough Questions to Ask When Interviewing Lawyers

1. **Are you experienced?** Don't be afraid to ask direct questions about a lawyer's experience. If you know you want to incorporate your business, for example, ask if he or she has ever handled an incorporation.
2. **Are you well connected?** Your business attorney should be something of a legal "internist"—one who can diagnose your problem, perform any "minor surgery" that may be needed, and refer you to local specialists for "major surgery" if needed. No lawyer can possibly know everything about every area of law. If your business has specialized legal needs (for example, a graphic designer may need someone who is familiar with copyright laws), your attorney should either be familiar with that special area or have a working relationship with someone who is. You shouldn't have to go scrounging for a new lawyer each time a different type of legal problem comes up.
3. **Do you have other clients in my industry?** Your attorney should be somewhat familiar with your industry and its legal environment. If not, he or she should be willing to learn the ins and outs of it. Scan your candidate's bookshelf or magazine rack for copies of the same journals and professional literature that you read. Be wary, however, of attorneys who represent one or more of your competitors. While the legal code of ethics requires that your lawyer keep everything you tell him or her strictly confidential, you do not want to risk an accidental leak of sensitive information to a competitor.
4. **Are you a good teacher?** Your attorney should be willing to take the time to educate you and your staff about the legal environment of your business. He or she should tell

you what the law says and explain how it affects the way you do business so that you can spot problems well in advance. The right lawyer will distribute such freebies as newsletters or memoranda that describe recent developments in the law affecting your business.

5. **Are you a finder, a minder, or a grinder?** Nearly every law firm has three types of lawyer. The "finder" scouts for business and brings in new clients; the "minder" takes on new clients and makes sure existing ones are happy; and the "grinder" does the clients' work. Your attorney should be a combination of a "minder" and a "grinder." If you sense that the lawyer you are talking to is not the one who will actually be doing your work, ask to meet the "grinder" and be sure you are comfortable with him or her.
6. **Will you be flexible in your billing?** Because there is currently a glut of lawyers, with far too many practicing in most geographic locales, lawyers are in a position to have to negotiate their fees as never before, and it is definitely a "buyer's market." Still, there are limits. Unlike the personal injury lawyers who advertise on television, business lawyers almost always will not work for a "contingency fee," payable only if your legal work is completed to your satisfaction.

Most lawyers will charge a flat one-time fee for routine matters, such as forming a corporation or LLC, but will not volunteer a flat fee unless you ask for it. Be sure to ask if the "flat fee" includes disbursements (the lawyer's out-of-pocket expenses, such as filing fees and overnight courier charges) and when the flat fee is expected to be paid. Many attorneys require payment of a flat fee up front, so that they can cover their out-of-pocket expenses. You should always ask to "hold back" 10 to 20 percent of a flat fee, though, in the event the lawyer doesn't do the job well.

Lawyers will be reluctant to quote flat fees if the matter involves litigation or negotiations with third parties. The reason for this is bluntly stated by a lawyer friend of mine: "Even though it's a transaction I've done dozens of times, if the other side's lawyer turns out to be a blithering idiot who wants to fight over every comma and semicolon in the contracts, then I can't control the amount of time I will be putting into the matter and will end up losing money if I quote a flat fee." In such situations, you will have to pay the lawyer's hourly rate. You should always ask for a written estimate of the amount of time involved and advance notice if circumstances occur that will cause the lawyer to exceed his or her estimate.

If a lawyer asks you for a retainer or deposit against future fees, make sure the money will be used and not held indefinitely in escrow and that the lawyer commits to return any unused portion of the retainer if the deal fails to close for any reason. You should be suspicious of any lawyer who offers to take an ownership interest in your business in lieu of a fee.

One last thing: don't forget to follow your instincts and feelings. You should be able to communicate openly and freely with your attorney at all times. If you feel you cannot trust a particular lawyer or you believe the two of you have different perspectives, keep looking. Just remember that *Ally McBeal*, *The Practice*, and *Boston Law* are not reality: good looks and a dynamic personality are not as important in a lawyer as accuracy, thoroughness, intelligence, the willingness to work hard for you, and attention to detail. As a former client once told me, "My father always said 'Never trust a lawyer who has 20/20 vision and wears Armani.' I chose you as my lawyer because you look like you work for a living." The right lawyer for your business will take that as a compliment.

Ten Ways to Drive Your Lawyer or Accountant Nuts

It's time to get some things off my chest.

Communicating with lawyers, accountants, and other professionals can sometimes be like talking to Martians. Professionals speak a different language, and a lot of them don't take the time to explain what they need in "plain English." Quite a few of them lack people skills of any kind.

Still, as a professional myself, I have to say that "it takes two" to mess up a relationship, and when professionals and clients fail to connect or communicate properly, the client is often at least partly to blame. Are you dissatisfied with the way your professionals perform? Before you switch, complain, withhold fees, or think about a malpractice suit, it may be worth some time to do some soul-searching and ask yourself if perhaps—just perhaps—you might be a problem client.

Here's my list of the ten most common ways small business clients drive their lawyers (accountants, insurance agents, or consultants) nuts:

#1: Forgetting that lawyers are businesspeople, too

Yes, we are professionals, and we are held to higher standards of competence and ethical behavior than most folks. We are often required by law to take on work we don't want to do. But we are also businesspeople, just like you. If you wouldn't do your job for $15 an hour, why would you seriously expect us to? A lot of clients expect me to spend entire weeks or months of my life working exclusively on their problem, putting all of my other clients off to one side, and they are shocked when they hear what I have to charge them for that kind of service. Never expect a professional to give you a better deal than you would give your own customers.

#2: Waiting until the last minute to call a lawyer

That lawsuit you've been chewing your nails about the last six months has finally happened. You have been served with a court summons that must be responded to within 10 days or you will forfeit your defense. Now, at long last, you call your attorney, only to hear on his voice mail recording that he is in the south of France for three weeks. You frantically grab the *Yellow Pages* and start calling other attorneys, only to hear the same thing over and over again—"We will need a retainer of $5,000 (or more) to take your case." It takes time to "get up to speed" on a matter when you've never worked with the client before! If you call a lawyer the night before he leaves on a three-week vacation with an emergency that forces him to postpone or cancel his vacation plans, do not expect a break on the fee.

#3: Expecting Park Avenue service for Wal-Mart rates

A good lawyer treats all clients as if they were her best client. But if every time you call a lawyer you insist that she drop everything she's doing and respond to your problem immediately, the lawyer will be asking herself "Is this client worth the pain?" If you are paying your lawyer only a couple of hundred dollars a year and she's got other clients who provide her with several thousand dollars a month, you should be prepared to be a little flexible in your demands. A good lawyer will always find the time to meet your real (not imagined) deadline if you show some basic respect for her time.

#4: Not being up-front about deadlines

Speaking of deadlines, you should always tell your lawyer when you need his response. We are very smart people, but we're not psychic. Lawyers need to juggle a lot of client demands, and it really helps when you say something like "I would like it by Wednesday, but I really need it by Friday for an important meeting." Leaving the deadline open-ended and then calling frantically the day you absolutely, positively need the response is sure to lead to disappointment.

#5: Playing the "gotcha" game

These days, when a lawyer talks to any client, the lawyer has one hand on her malpractice insurance policy. Sending a lawyer the message that she's "only as good as her first mistake" or that you cannot wait to sue her for malpractice should she ever slip up, even in a small way, is likely to cause the lawyer to think "this one's not worth the risk," and she will refer you to another lawyer—probably her worst enemy.

#6: Not responding promptly to requests for information

Working with a lawyer is a give-and-take proposition. If a lawyer asks you questions and it takes you three weeks to pull together the information she needs, while ignoring her follow-up phone calls, don't blame the lawyer for missing deadlines! Also, you should have no secrets from your lawyer—everything you tell her must be true, accurate, and complete to the best of your knowledge. If you lie to your lawyer or leave out important information when you present your situation to her, the lawyer (in most states) can terminate your relationship with impunity and leave you hanging.

#7: Not confirming a fee quote in writing

Whenever a lawyer quotes a fee, it should always be in writing, just like any other legal contract. Mistakes and misunderstandings happen all the time here, and it benefits both of you to be crystal clear about the fees you will pay and when you will be required to pay them. For example, there's a big difference between an estimated fee ("I think this project will take about two hours") and a discounted or limited fee ("I won't bill

you for more than two hours on this project"). If your budget is limited, you should let your lawyer know up front.

#8: Overnegotiating the fee

When looking for a lawyer, there's no harm in shopping around to get the best deal you can. If you think a lawyer is charging too much, you should bring to his attention that other lawyers quoted you a lower fee. Lawyers have lots of competition these days, and they're highly motivated to give you the best deal they can. But don't go overboard. Most lawyers soon find that clients who haggle over every penny of every bill are simply not worth having.

#9: "Sandbagging" the lawyer

Clients sometimes "sandbag" their attorneys by negotiating a discounted fee and then hitting them with a much larger, more complex job than the attorney was led to believe. Recently a client called and asked me if I would help him negotiate a simple lease of retail space in a local strip mall. I quoted my standard $500 fee for negotiating a simple lease. He accepted and then sent me an e-mail with thirty-six issues he wanted me to negotiate with the landlord, "plus anything else you find when you do your legal review of the lease." Needless to say, this would have required much more time than a $500 fee would justify. What did I do? I called the client back and said that while my $500 quote for the legal review was still firm, I would have to charge extra for "negotiating business issues, which are normally the client's responsibility." The client grumbled but agreed.

#10: Sending important messages via e-mail

E-mail is an extremely potent and convenient tool, but it has its limitations. There are still a lot of "bugs" to be worked

out, especially when it comes to security issues. You should never do any of the following things:

- » Communicate sensitive personal information (such as your Social Security Number or your business tax ID number) to your lawyer by e-mail.
- » Use e-mail to conduct delicate and detailed negotiations, where facial expressions and tone of voice can communicate a lot of information that mere words cannot.
- » Say anything in an e-mail that you would want to be treated as a "privileged attorney-client communication" in the event of a lawsuit.

Don't be surprised if your attorney refuses to communicate with you at all via e-mail; if she does, it's not because she's "behind the times." It's because she's being careful and is looking out for your best interests—isn't that, after all, what you are paying her for?

CHAPTER 12

YOURSELF: "I HAVE MET THE ENEMY, AND IT IS ME"

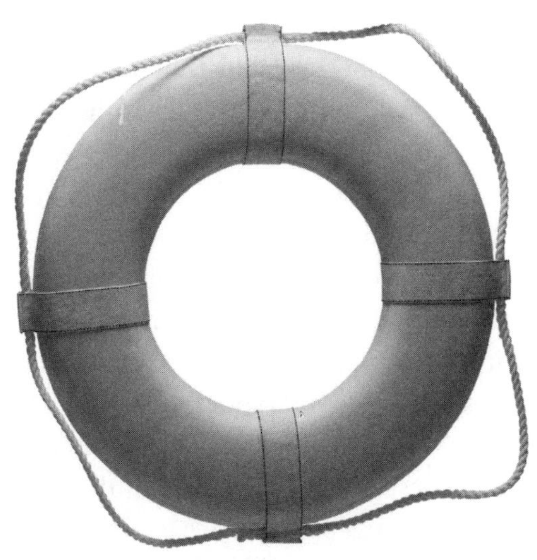

The one absolutely essential personality trait of the entrepreneur is self-confidence. If you don't believe in yourself, if you don't have a strong ego bordering on arrogance, success in business is virtually impossible. Getting from "I am going to do this someday" to "This is already happening; I am doing this today" requires faith in your own knowledge, experience, and judgment that most of us humble folks find it hard to muster. Ever wonder why it is that so many highly successful people are so conceited, cocky, and extraordinarily vain about their image that they become easy targets for pundits, cartoonists, and late-night television comedians? I will let you in on a secret: they didn't just get that way after they made their first million dollars.

Like everything else in life, self-confidence comes at a price, and if you are not willing to pay that price, you leave yourself and your business open to the most pernicious enemy of them all: yourself. When I was eighteen years old, I thought (like all eighteen-year-old people) that I could do anything I set my mind to. All I had to do was read a few books and look at people closely enough, and I could adapt to any situation quickly, effortlessly, without friction. Hard and painful experience has taught me over the years (as it does everyone sooner or later) that my eighteen-year-old view of the world was not true. Try as I might, no matter how many books I read or how much experience I have, there are certain things I just cannot do, was never meant to do, and never will be able to do.

When you are self-confident, the hardest thing in life is to acknowledge that you have limitations, faults, and weaknesses. In fact, to protect your business against others, it is absolutely essential that you hide your limitations, faults, and weaknesses; as far as your enemies are concerned, you must appear to be the meanest, toughest, person on the playing field and about as easy to mess with as a pack of feral rottweilers. Martha

Stewart is in a creative, delicate, and largely feminine business, but no one on earth would call her a wallflower—not to her face in any event. But you must never be taken in by your self-image. That is for the outside world—your "poker face." You must see yourself the way you really are; otherwise your self-image becomes the biggest challenge to your success.

Dealing with Your "Inner Employee"

Back in the 1980s, there was a flurry of books and articles advising people to get in touch with their "inner child." The idea was that, as we grow older, we tend to get set in our ways and need to remind ourselves of the childhood dreams, spontaneity, and sense of fun that launched us into the adult world.

Let's talk about another little person that lives inside your skull. Psychologists have a fancy name for him or her (of course, it's really an "it"), but I like to think of it as your "inner employee."

Picture this. In a tiny cubicle in your brain there lives an employee—a miniature version of you. Like any employee, it cannot do whatever it wants—it works for you. Its mission in life is to help you get what you want.

So let's say you're not having fun with your business. You are unhappy; you dread going to the office every day. You say to yourself, over and over again, "I want out of this business. I would do anything to get out of this business." Well, guess what? Your inner employee picks up on this message and says, "Gee, the boss really wants to get out of this business. What creative ways can I come up with to help the boss achieve this goal?"

Have you ever found yourself doing something truly stupid in your business—making a mistake that not even an amateur would make? Like most of us, you probably have. When it happens, you slap yourself on the forehead and say something

like "Gee, how could I have been so stupid?" In many cases, you were not stupid at all. Rather, you have been sending your inner employee negative messages, and your inner employee came up with a creative (sometimes truly ingenious) way for you to screw up and perhaps lose your business.

You shouldn't get mad at your inner employee when you do stupid things. It is only doing its job, after all. You did say you would do anything to get out of the business, right?

You can sometimes bargain with your inner employee. If you find yourself in a truly unpleasant position, you can say "Hey, inner employee, I know what I'm doing now really stinks, but I need you to help me get through it for the next few months, until the end of the year. If things don't work out by then, I promise I'll get out." Your inner employee will work with you as long as you stick to your end of the bargain. Just don't try to do a "snow job" on your inner employee. Your inner employee has a memory like an elephant and will trip you up if it senses you are not being true to yourself.

Because the inner employee lives inside your head, you cannot fire or downsize it. It works tirelessly twenty-four hours a day. You can, however, change the inner employee's marching orders and get it working in a positive direction.

For example, let's say you are truly happy with your business. You have a few problems, but there's no question in your mind you are a "fit" for what you do, enjoy the work, and find it satisfying overall. You find yourself saying over and over again "Gee, I love this business, but I wish I could do X better. I wish I could increase my revenue or profits by Y percent."

Your inner employee listens to these messages and acts accordingly. Have you ever labored long and hard over a difficult problem, only to have the absolutely perfect solution suddenly pop into your head, seemingly out of nowhere, when you weren't even thinking about it? That's not luck or coincidence. That's your inner employee working overtime on the problem, even when you weren't. When this happens, you should give your inner employee a bonus—mine is partial to cherry cheesecake.

Never Let Them See You Bleed

I played high school football for all of two weeks. I was a rather large teenager—6 foot and 225 pounds, and my high school football team didn't have that many large teenagers. As a result, the football coach was always nagging me to try out for the team. I gave in after awhile, partly out of curiosity and a feeling that "if I don't try it now, I'll never know if I would be any good at it."

At my request, the coach tried me out in all of the "glamour" positions on the team—quarterback, fullback, tight end, but there was no perfect fit for me. I was too slow to be a fullback, too tentative to be a tight end, and didn't have the arm to be a quarterback. As I struggled through scrimmage after scrimmage, I found myself being pushed by the coaches into the offensive line.

For those of you who don't know football, the offensive line is the least glamorous place to be on a football team. Your sole mission in life is to prevent the other side's defensive players—who are always bigger and stronger than you—from killing your team's quarterback before he can move the ball where it needs to go. Watch any football game on television, and I guarantee the offensive linemen are the ones covered head to toe in mud (or even blood) so badly you can't even read their numbers.

I hated being on the offensive line. That is why I quit after two weeks. But that's not the important point.

The important point is what I learned during those two weeks. When I first was assigned to the offensive line, the coach told me, in the strident tone of a Marine drill sergeant, "Cliff,

there's only one thing you gotta know about being in the line. When you get into position, you gotta check out your opponent on the other team—the guy you are going to hit. Look at him carefully all over. Look for bandages, knee braces, athletic supports—anything that will tell you he's hurting somewhere. And when you see he's got them and the quarterback calls "hup hup," make sure you keep hitting those places over and over again until he goes down and doesn't come up again. Then do the same thing to the next guy they put opposite you. And the next. And while you're doing this, make damn sure that other guy doesn't see your bandages, knee braces, athletic supports, or anything else that'll help him wipe you off the field. Do these things, and you'll be all-state."

Not surprisingly, I never was all-state, but I learned a powerful lesson about life in the business world. In a tough, competitive environment, whether you are male or female, Type A or Type B, you cannot let the enemy see your weaknesses. You cannot show insecurity, fear, lack of knowledge, lack of experience, or any "bandages, knee braces, or athletic supports" that will make it easier for your enemy to wipe you off the field. They must believe that you have superhuman strength and will fight like a pit bull if challenged even slightly. Because business, like football, is an unforgiving game, your enemy will not hesitate to hit you where you are weakest because that's where they know you will hit them (and you will, won't you?) if they give you half a chance. This sounds like tough advice, but if you care enough about protecting your business, it's easier than you think.

Know Your Weaknesses

While it is essential in business to make sure others don't see your weaknesses, you must never let it get to the point that you don't believe you have any. Sometimes the biggest enemy you have in business is reality, and it's utterly ruthless. You always have to know where reality is at any given moment; if you take your eyes off it for any length of time, it has a nasty habit of catching you by surprise.

The ancient Greeks used to say that "knowing yourself" is the beginning of wisdom. I prefer to say that being brutally honest with yourself about your own limitations, weaknesses, and shortcomings—and developing strategies to overcome them—is the first step to business success. You must look for weaknesses in yourself with the same intensity that you look for weaknesses in others.

One of the most common ways business owners get in the way of their own success is by staying on the job too long. The skills required to start a business are, very often, not the skills that are required to build and grow the business. Sooner or later, a company grows to the point where people can no longer run the business; management systems must be developed to run the business, with people responsible for running and improving the systems. Making the transition from entrepreneur to manager requires a seismic shift in style, talent, and personality that few of us can manage successfully. Even if you can do so, you probably won't enjoy what you have to do day to day. Sooner or later that lack of enjoyment will turn into lack of motivation, and you will find yourself on a downwardly spiraling curve.

Yet, most entrepreneurs become emotionally attached to their businesses, and as with any child that is ready to fly out of the nest, it's awfully hard to let go. Staying at the top too long and ignoring the fact that the business has outgrown your capabilities makes you the enemy of your own success. Let go, keep a good percentage of the company stock, take a trip around the world for six months, and start something new.

Avoiding "Willy Loman Syndrome"

For my birthday a couple of years ago, my wife took me to see a Broadway revival of Arthur Miller's classic tragedy *Death of a Salesman*. I find I get a lot more out of a theatrical performance if I've read through the play a day or two before seeing it; so I went to the library and checked out their dog-eared paperback of *Death of a Salesman*.

As I read the play, I found that the central character of Willy Loman was surprisingly familiar to me. He reminded me of many of my law clients—founders of small businesses, most of them working alone out of their homes, and many of them forced into entrepreneurship because of corporate downsizings and other circumstances beyond their control. When I went to the play and saw actor Brian Dennehy's spectacular performance as Willy, I realized that in working with entrepreneurs for almost twenty years I have met Willy Loman time and time again. He no longer wears a suit and tie, no longer lugs around heavy sample cases, and no longer has three-martini lunches with department store buyers, but he is very much alive and with us today. You, too, will meet him (or her) and may become Willy Loman yourself if you are not careful.

In a nutshell, *Death of a Salesman* is a Greek tragedy about the downfall and eventual suicide of one Willy Loman—an unsuccessful traveling salesman (what we would today call a manufacturer's rep), failed husband and father, relentless dreamer, and American Everyman. If you are starting your own business or thinking about it, here are some lessons from *Death of a Salesman*:

LESSON #1: Don't Believe Your Own B.S.

Willy Loman is a man who has been selling for so long that he has lost his grip on reality. His ability to "spin" things in the most positive manner possible and overcome all objections from customers has carried over into his personal life, and he is unable to grasp some unpleasant truths: that his two sons are losers (one a convicted felon) who will never achieve anything in life, that he has "burned out" in his job and that his employer is quietly looking to replace him, and that he has been subconsciously trying to commit suicide by a succession of one-car "accidents" on isolated country roads.

Willy, however, presents himself to the world as a successful businessman with a perfect family and powerful friends throughout his sales territory who will gladly travel hundreds of miles to come to his funeral. Even when the truth is eventually presented to Willy in starkly clear terms, he stubbornly refuses to accept it and clings to his dream like an alcoholic clutching a bottle.

To be successful, entrepreneurs have to sell every day. As the song says, they must "accentuate the positive, eliminate the negative, and watch out for Mr. In-Between." In the words of the play: "A salesman has got to dream, boy; it comes with the territory." Successful selling sometimes means stretching the truth a little bit and building a "castle in the air" you hope prospective customers will believe in. Unfortunately, you cannot afford the luxury of living in the air castles you create. Your employees, friends, and family (sometimes even your customers and suppliers) won't tell you the truth because they want to keep their jobs, your friendship, and your love and accordingly will tell you only what you want to hear. Maybe they, too, have been "sold" and want to believe in your dream so badly they share in your fantasy and start tuning out the unpleasant news coming in from the real world that will ultimately crush you.

LESSON #2: Sometimes the People Who Stand in Your Way Are the Ones Who Love You

Willy's wife Linda helps to keep Willy in the dark about what's actually going on in his world. As it turns out, she is

also one of the main reasons Willy never pursued his youthful entrepreneurial dreams. In a flashback scene, Willy's older brother Ben—a highly successful entrepreneur—offers Willy the chance to join him in a timberland venture in Alaska (a venture we later learn was highly successful). Willy is eager to join Ben, but Willy's wife upbraids Ben: "Don't say those things to [Willy]! Enough to be happy right here, right now. Why must everybody conquer the world? You're well liked, and the boys love you, and someday . . ."

One of the most difficult truths about running your own business is that it requires total concentration of body, mind, and soul—at least for awhile. You must be willing to take terrible chances and do things that will make those closest to you wonder if you've lost your marbles. The cost of such concentration and risk-taking may be high—the alienation of family members and friends, the loss of hobbies and leisure pastimes you may not be able to resume in later life—but must be paid. Too many failed entrepreneurs have fallen by the wayside, like Willy, because they cared too much about what other people—people whose opinions they valued—thought of them and ended up staying in a job that they knew would not get them what they really wanted out of life.

LESSON #3: Find Out What Works and Keep Doing It

Despite Willy's faith in the power of personality, Willy is mystified about what actually causes someone to be successful. He idolizes his brother Ben, the entrepreneur who at age seventeen sailed to Africa, went into the jungle, and came out at twenty-one a millionaire. However, we never find out—because Willy doesn't know—what Ben did in the jungle that led to his success. Clearly, Ben found "something he could sell" in the jungle—gold, ivory, diamonds, or some other commodity—and worked hard to exploit it during his four years in Africa.

Success in business is never a mystery. You provide something—a product, a service, a new way of marketing or distributing products and services—that people need or want enough to pay good money for. If that something works (i.e., if people are buying it), you work like the devil to get the message out. If that something does not work, you leave it behind and move on to something else. If you don't know what that something is, you are not in business.

Building a Board of Advisors

No single individual can possibly hope to make perfect business decisions all the time. We all have ideas, intuitions, and impulses, but we need to check them against reality to be sure the world really works the way we perceive it does. One of a small businessperson's first tasks is to set up a Board of Advisors to meet regularly (either live in person or by telephone conference call) to review the monthly or quarterly operating results, ask difficult questions, share advice, and perhaps make some personal contacts to help the business move forward. There should be at least five people on your Board of Advisors:

Your accountant or bookkeeper—No one knows your business numbers like your accountant, CPA, or bookkeeper. If you see your accountant only at tax time and then only to help you fill out your tax returns, you are wasting a valuable resource.

Your lawyer—Most small businesses wait until they are being sued before they look for an attorney. This is a bad mistake. The time to hire an attorney is before the wolf is at the door—to help you with the contracts and other protective devices that are available to prevent lawsuits and regulatory actions (such as tax audits) before they happen.

An insurance agent or benefits planner—Entrepreneurs sometimes get so busy building their business that they forget to provide for themselves and their families. An expert who can advise on reasonable compensation for you and your employees, suitable and affordable benefit programs, and financial and estate planning is worth his or her weight in platinum.

A mentor—I don't care how "high tech" or "dot-com" your business is; someone's been there and done that before you. Check your industry organization, chamber of commerce, or SCORE (Service Corps of Retired Executives) chapter for a retired entrepreneur in the same or a related business. They're out there, and they will be only too happy to get out of the house and meet with you once a week. Everybody makes mistakes, but why should you make the same ones everyone else makes?

Your spouse, significant other, or a loved one—I'm not suggesting that you bring in your spouse, significant other, or loved one as a business partner. Entrepreneurs often forget about the impact their businesses have on their personal lives and fail to communicate to their spouses or significant others the pressures they are under. As a result, misunderstandings build up that often prove fatal to both the relationship and the business. It's helpful for your spouse, significant other, or loved one to know enough about your business that (A) they will understand and empathize more with the pressures you are under, which in turn will take pressure off of your relationship, and (B) they will be in a position to tell you when you are about to take an action that will have an adverse impact on your relationship. Besides, the monthly advisors' meeting may be their only chance to see you!

Once you have formed a Board of Advisors, keep in touch with them, either individually or in a regularly scheduled meeting, on a frequent basis (monthly or quarterly is customary). This will help you build "reality checking" into your business planning process and help you spot problems before it's too late to change course.

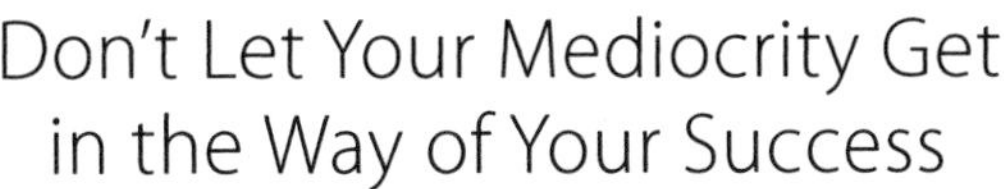

Don't Let Your Mediocrity Get in the Way of Your Success

As a fan of musical humorists like Victor Borge and Spike Jones, I recently bought a CD entitled *Murder on the High C's: Florence Foster Jenkins & Friends, Original Recordings 1937–1951.* The liner notes to the Naxos recording promised "the complete recordings of the 'Dire Diva' . . . not to mention several offerings by people who should have known better." I couldn't wait to listen to it.

You've never heard of Florence Foster Jenkins? I'm not surprised. Many classical music aficionados have never heard of her, and many of those who have wish they hadn't. The truth is that nobody knows much about Florence Foster Jenkins, except that:

- She was a wealthy New York City socialite during the 1920s and 1930s, who died in 1944 at the age of approximately seventy-five (her exact date of birth is not known).
- She founded and guided the Verdi Club (an opera fan club of wealthy socialites) for thirty years.
- She loved to sing.

We know she loved singing because at her death she left behind about ten 78 rpm records, made sometime during the early 1940s, on which she sings some of the most famous soprano arias from the great operas, accompanied by

an excellent pianist credited as Cosme McMoon (frankly, it sounds like a phony name meant to hide the identity of a well-known performer helping out an old friend). We also know that once a year she rented the ballroom of New York's Ritz-Carlton Hotel to give a private concert for her friends and fellow Verdi Club members.

These recordings were private pressings ("self-published," we would say today) made at Ms. Jenkins's own expense and distributed to her friends and family members as holiday gifts. Having listened to the CD compiling them several times now, I can tell you one thing about Florence Foster Jenkins—the lady couldn't sing to save her soul. These recordings are not the work of a great musician who is consciously having some fun with the classics to show how good she really is. On each song, Florence Foster Jenkins is truly, majestically awful. She sings at least two keys flat, misses almost all of the high notes by a country mile, is either way behind or far ahead of her piano accompanist, tires audibly about halfway through each song, and finishes up by yapping like a Park Avenue poodle chasing a squirrel in Central Park.

These recordings are guaranteed to make your dog howl; your cat will disappear under the sofa for weeks. If you have a teenager in the house who plays Eminem at top volume all day, I can think of little better revenge than to give him or her a dose of Florence Foster Jenkins.

Yet, after I listened to the first Jenkins song on the recording, I laughed, when I wasn't wincing in pain. By the second song, I felt pity for the old gal, trying so hard to hit the notes with lots of heart but zero talent—I mean, even a novice singer gets at least half the notes right. I was also a little angry at her friends and Verdi Club pals who egged her on and led her to believe, despite the evidence, that she was on a par with the great opera sopranos of her time. By the third, fourth, and fifth song, I realized something amazing—as horrible a singer as Florence Foster Jenkins was, I couldn't stop listening to this recording. Something about it was keeping me glued to my CD player.

What it was, I realized after awhile, was Jenkins's sheer presence. She was not doing this for laughs. She clearly loved what she was doing (an "amateur"—one who loves—in the truest sense of that word) and couldn't have cared less about what I, or anyone else, thought. By the fifth song I was rooting for her, hoping and praying for her to succeed this time, and when she did hit one of the high notes dead on target (which she does about 5 percent of the time), I almost wanted to pump my fist in the air and yell "Attagirl!" Her mediocrity is majestic, almost noble. You gotta love her.

So what does all of this have to do with running your own home-based business?

Many of us Baby Boomers who have started our own businesses have entered our fifties, and it has become painfully apparent to most of us that our youthful ambitions of changing the world will never be achieved. We have to face the fact that we are now "over the hill," and for most of us, greatness is just as far away as it was when we were in our twenties.

I remember one of my professors in law school, then in his own fifties, telling us about how we would feel when we reached his age: "You are all very bright young men and women, the cream of America's top colleges. But let me tell you something. No matter how good you are, no matter how hard you work, the simple fact is that the Bell Curve applies to all aspects of life, and the vast majority of you—90 percent or more—are destined to be stuck in the middle. You will not fail, but you will not achieve truly great things either. You will never argue a case before the Supreme Court, become a top judge, or occupy a high elective office. You will find yourself in a small to medium-sized town, writing wills, buying and selling houses,

representing small clients in court on small cases, and helping people start and shut down small businesses. Maybe you will sit on the local Board of Education or run unsuccessfully for mayor. You will do a lot of good for your clients, but no one will ever erect a statue of you in the town square or name a building after you. I don't mean to burst your bubble, but that's just how it is, statistically speaking."

Somehow I don't think my old law professor and Florence Foster Jenkins would have gotten along at all. I don't think he would have understood a seventy-year-old woman, with her life pretty much behind her and not much in the way of achievement to show for it, plunking down serious money to make some records and realize a childhood dream of becoming a great opera singer, with no hope of success. Making some truly horrible recordings, to be sure, but having the time of her life doing it. A woman whose records are still selling more than fifty years after her death, probably more than any of the "real" opera stars of her time, and inspiring that 99.9 percent of us who will never play a role at the Metropolitan Opera or solo on *American Idol* (a show where Florence might have fit right in, come to think of it).

There are a few Enrico Carusos in the world of small business, but there are a lot more Florence Foster Jenkinses. If you are not destined for greatness but instead for only modest success, you can still achieve it with style, flamboyance, dignity, and pride and let the critics be damned. Let people see the passion that keeps you going at it every day, even though you know you will never be one of the greats. Keep straining to hit those high Cs because every once in a blue moon you will indeed hit one, and posterity will take notice.

APPENDIX

SAMPLE BUSINESS FORMS, DOCUMENTS, AND CLAUSES

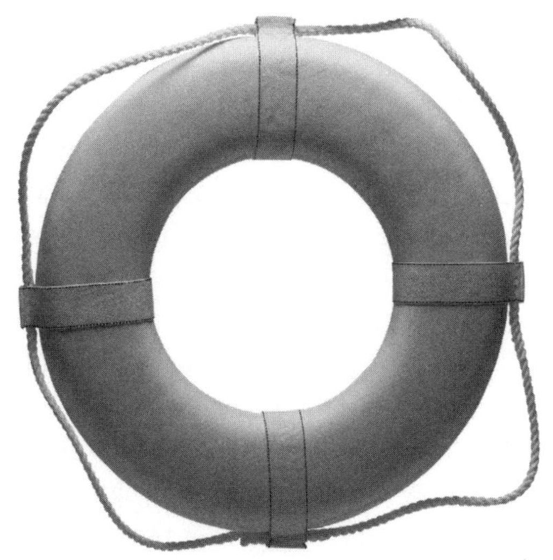

Form 1: Mutual Nondisclosure Agreement

Form 2: Assignment of Rights Clause

Form 3: Employee Noncompete and Nondisclosure Agreement

Form 4: Offer of Employment

Form 5: "Earn-In" Clause

Form 6: "Golden Rule" or "Russian Roulette" Buyout Clause

Form 7: "Supermajority Voting" Clause

Form 8: "Management and Control" Clause

FORM 1: MUTUAL NONDISCLOSURE AGREEMENT

THIS AGREEMENT (this "Agreement") is entered into on or as of the ____ day of __________, 2____, by and between ____________________, a [corporation/partnership/limited liability company] having offices located at ____________________________________ ("Company"), and ____________________, a [corporation/partnership/limited liability company] having offices located at ____________________________________ ("Customer");

WITNESSETH:

WHEREAS, the parties hereto acknowledge that certain trade secrets and confidential or nonpublic information of a party hereto may be disclosed to the other party hereto in connection with Company's engagement by Customer to provide certain services to or for the benefit of Customer;

NOW, THEREFORE, in consideration of the foregoing and the mutual promises set forth herein, the parties hereto hereby agree as follows:

1. Definition. "Confidential Information" of a party hereto shall be deemed to include all information, materials and data disclosed or supplied by such party ("Disclosing Party") to the other party hereto receiving such information, materials or data ("Receiving Party"), that Disclosing Party designates to be of a confidential nature. If disclosed in written or other tangible form or electronically, Confidential Information shall be marked by Disclosing Party as "Confidential." If disclosed orally or visually, Confidential Information shall be identified as such by Disclosing Party at the time of disclosure and designated as "Confidential" in a written memorandum of such disclosure, summarizing the Confidential Information sufficiently for identification, to be delivered by Disclosing Party to Receiving Party within thirty (30) days of such disclosure.

2. Exceptions. The following information shall not be considered Confidential Information hereunder: (1) information of Disclosing Party that is or becomes generally known within the relevant industry through no wrongful act or omission of Receiving Party or breach by Receiving Party of Receiving Party's obligations under this Agreement; (2) information which Receiving Party can establish and document by contemporaneous written proof was in the possession of or known by Receiving Party prior to Receiving Party's receipt of such information from Disclosing Party, without any obligation of confidentiality to Disclosing Party; (3) information that is rightfully disclosed to Receiving Party by a third party with no obligation of confidentiality to Disclosing Party; and (4) information which is independently developed by Receiving

Party without use of or reference to Confidential Information of Disclosing Party, with Receiving Party bearing the burden of proving such independent development. To the extent Receiving Party is required to disclose Confidential Information of Disclosing Party pursuant to any court or regulatory order, Receiving Party shall promptly notify Disclosing Party in writing of the existence, terms and circumstances surrounding such disclosure so that Disclosing Party may seek a protective order or other appropriate remedy from the proper authority. Receiving Party agrees to cooperate with Disclosing Party in seeking such order or remedy. Receiving Party further agrees that if Receiving Party is required to disclose Confidential Information of Disclosing Party, Receiving Party shall furnish only that portion of Confidential Information that is legally required and shall exercise all reasonable efforts to obtain reliable, written assurances that confidential treatment shall be accorded Confidential Information.

3. Use and Protection. Confidential Information of Disclosing Party may not be used by Receiving Party for any purpose except in the performance of Receiving Party's obligations on behalf of and as directed by Disclosing Party and engaged in related discussions with Disclosing Party. Receiving Party shall maintain the confidentiality of all of Disclosing Party's Confidential Information disclosed to Receiving Party hereunder and shall not disclose such Confidential Information to any person or entity, except as provided in this Agreement. Receiving Party shall: (a) hold Disclosing Party's Confidential Information in confidence with the same degree of care with which Receiving Party protects Receiving Party's own confidential or proprietary information, but no less than reasonable care; (b) restrict disclosure of Disclosing Party's Confidential information solely to Receiving Party's employees with a legitimate need to know such Confidential Information and advise

such employees of their obligations hereunder with respect to such Confidential Information; and (c) use Disclosing Party's Confidential Information only as needed for the purpose of carrying out Receiving Party's duties as an independent contractor on behalf of and as directed by Disclosing Party.

4. Return of Confidential Information. Receiving Party shall promptly return to Disclosing Party all correspondence, memoranda, papers, files, records and other tangible materials embodying Disclosing Party's Confidential Information or from which such information may be derived, including all copies, extracts or other reproductions thereof, when Receiving Party no longer needs such Confidential Information to accomplish the performance of Receiving Party's obligations on behalf of Disclosing Party or when Disclosing Party requests its return, whichever occurs first, or certify to Disclosing Party that all such materials have been destroyed if Disclosing Party requests such destruction. Without limiting the generality of the foregoing, the obligation to promptly return Disclosing Party's Confidential Information shall include, but not be limited to, the obligation to promptly erase any and all of such Confidential Information, and all images, compilations, copies, summaries or abstracts of such information, from computer storage, systems and related storage devices, tools and servers of Receiving Party.

5. Equitable Relief. A breach by a party hereto of the provisions of this Agreement cannot reasonably or adequately be compensated in damages in an action at law and shall cause irreparable harm and significant injury and damage to the other party hereto. By reason thereof, the aggrieved party hereto shall be entitled, in addition to any other remedies such party may have under this Agreement or otherwise, to seek and obtain immediate preliminary, interim and permanent injunctive or

other equitable relief to prevent or curtail any actual or threatened breach of the provisions of this Agreement.

6. Relationship of the Parties. This Agreement shall not create, nor shall be represented by either party hereto to create, a partnership, joint venture, employer-employee, master-servant, principal-agent, or other relationship whatsoever between the parties hereto.

7. Successors and Assigns. This Agreement shall benefit and be binding upon the parties hereto and their respective successors and assigns.

8. Modification or Waiver. The parties hereto may, by mutual agreement, amend any provision of this Agreement, and any party hereto may grant consent or waive any right to which such party is entitled under this Agreement or any condition to such party's obligations under this Agreement, provided that each such amendment, consent or waiver shall be in writing.

9. Governing Law. This Agreement shall be governed by and construed in accordance with the laws of the State of ____________________ and the federal laws of the United States of America. The parties hereto consent to submit to the exclusive jurisdiction and venue of the courts of the State of ____________________, or the federal courts of the United States of America located in the City of ____________________ and State of ____________________, for any actions, suits or proceedings arising out of or relating to this Agreement.

10. Severability. In the event that any provision of this Agreement, or any word, phrase, clause, sentence or other provision thereof, should be held to be unenforceable or

invalid for any reason, such provision or portion thereof shall be modified or deleted in such a manner so as to make this Agreement as modified legal and enforceable to the fullest extent permitted under applicable law.

11. Counterparts. This Agreement may be executed in multiple counterparts, each of which shall be deemed to be an original, but all of which shall together constitute one and the same instrument.

IN WITNESS WHEREOF the parties hereto have caused this Agreement to be duly executed by their respective officers thereunto duly authorized, and delivered as of the date first above written.

[NAME OF COMPANY]

By: ______________________________

Print Name and Title:

ACCEPTED AND AGREED:

[NAME OF CUSTOMER]

By: ______________________________

Print Name and Title:

FORM 2: ASSIGNMENT OF RIGHTS CLAUSE

1. ASSIGNMENT. All the Consultant's rights, title and interest to inventions, whether patentable or unpatentable, software, computer programs. Firmware, manuals, mask works, improvements, developments, trademarks, service marks, trade times and designs (collectively "Intellectual Property") which, during the period of the Consultant's engagement by Company, the Consultant has made developed or conceived or hereafter may make, develop or conceive, either solely or jointly with others,

   1.1 with the use of Company's time, materials, or facilities, or

   1.2 resulting from or suggested by the Consultant's work for Company, or

   1.3 which, at least in part, arise from or are related to the Consultant's work assignments, or to information obtained from Company or its customers in the course of the Consultant's engagement, is hereby assigned to and is the exclusive property of Company, and shall be promptly disclosed to Company and its successors, and assigns.

2. DISCLOSURE. The Consultant shall make and maintain adequate and current written records of all such Intellectual Property in the form of notes, sketches, drawings, or reports relating thereto; which records shall be and remain the property of and available to Company at all times and the Consultant shall promptly disclose to Company all such Intellectual Property.

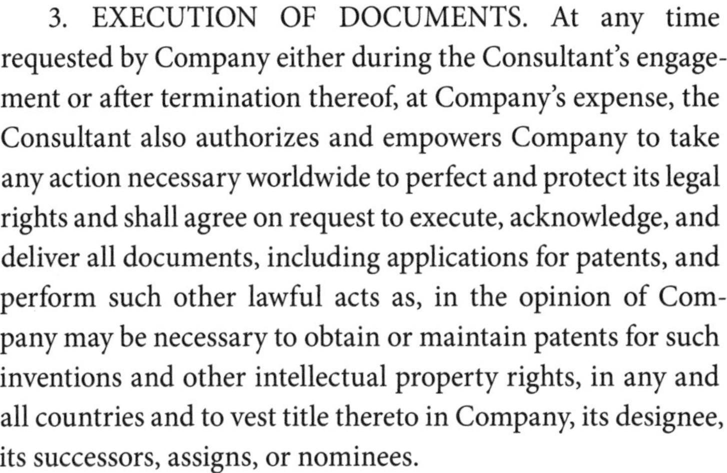

3. EXECUTION OF DOCUMENTS. At any time requested by Company either during the Consultant's engagement or after termination thereof, at Company's expense, the Consultant also authorizes and empowers Company to take any action necessary worldwide to perfect and protect its legal rights and shall agree on request to execute, acknowledge, and deliver all documents, including applications for patents, and perform such other lawful acts as, in the opinion of Company may be necessary to obtain or maintain patents for such inventions and other intellectual property rights, in any and all countries and to vest title thereto in Company, its designee, its successors, assigns, or nominees.

FORM 3: EMPLOYEE NONCOMPETE AND NONDISCLOSURE AGREEMENT

In consideration of my being a ____________________ [describe title] of ____________________ (the "Employer"), and other good and valuable consideration, the receipt and sufficiency of which is acknowledged, I hereby acknowledge and agree that:

1. ____________________, a [corporation/partnership/limited liability company] having offices at ____________________ (the "Employer") establishes and operates a ____________________ business (the "Business") and the right to use in the operation of the Business the Employer's unique and distinctive format and system relating to the establishment and operation of the Business (the "System"), as they may be changed, improved and further developed from time to time in the Employer's sole discretion.

2. The Employer possesses certain proprietary and confidential information relating to the operation of the System, which includes certain proprietary methods, techniques, formats, specifications, systems, procedures, methods of business practices and management, sales and promotional techniques and knowledge of, and experience in, the operation of the Business, as well as client, customer, employee, subcontractor and contact lists (the "Confidential Information").

3. In addition to the above, any and all information, knowledge, know-how, and techniques that the Employer specifically designates as confidential shall be deemed to be Confidential Information for purposes of this Agreement.

4. To assist me in the performance of my duties for the Employer, the Employer will disclose the Confidential

Information to me in furnishing training and general assistance to me during the term of this Agreement.

5. I will not acquire any interest in the Confidential Information, other than the right to utilize it in the operation of the Business during the term hereof, and the use or duplication of the Confidential Information for any use outside the System would constitute an unfair method of competition.

6. The Confidential Information is proprietary, involves trade secrets of the Employer, and is disclosed to me solely on the condition that I agree that I shall hold in strict confidence all Confidential Information and all other information designed by the Employer as confidential, and will not use Confidential Information in any manner detrimental to the interests of Employer. Unless the Employer otherwise agrees in writing, I will use the Confidential Information only in connection with my duties for the Employer, and will continue not to disclose or use any such information even after I cease to be in that position unless I can demonstrate that such information has become generally known or easily accessible to the general public other than by the breach of my obligations under this Agreement.

7. Except as otherwise approved in writing by the Employer, I shall not, while in my position with the Employer and for a continuous uninterrupted period commencing upon the cessation or termination of my position with Employer, regardless of the cause for termination, and continuing for two (2) years thereafter, either directly or indirectly, for myself, or through, on behalf of, or in conjunction with any person, persons, partnership, limited liability company, corporation or other business entity, (A) directly or indirectly solicit business or employment from any employee, agent, subcontractor, customer or client of the Employer during the term of my employment, or (B) own, maintain, operate, engage in, act as a consultant for, perform

services for, be employed by, or have any interest in any business substantially similar to, or competitive with, the present business of the Employer or such other business activity in which the Employer may substantially engage during the term of my employment, which is or is intended to be, located within the State or Connecticut or within one hundred (100) miles of the Employer's location. This restriction does not apply to my ownership of less than 5% beneficial interest in the outstanding securities of any publicly held corporation.

8. I agree that each of the foregoing covenants shall be constructed as independent of any other covenant or provision of this Agreement. If all or any portion of a covenant in this Agreement is held unreasonable or unenforceable by a court or agency having valid jurisdiction in an unappealed final decision to which the Employer is a party, I expressly agree to be bound by any lesser covenant subsumed within the terms of such covenant that imposes the maximum duty by law, as if the resulting covenant were separately stated in and made part of this Agreement.

9. I understand and acknowledge that the Employer shall have the right, in its sole discretion, to reduce the scope of any covenant set forth in this Agreement, or any portion thereof, without my consent, effective immediately upon receipt by me of written notice thereof; and I agree to comply forthwith with any covenant as so modified.

10. I am aware that my violation of this Agreement will cause the Employer irreparable harm; therefore, I acknowledge and agree that the Employer may apply for the issuance of an injunction preventing me from violating this Agreement, and I agree to pay the Employer all the costs it incurs, including, without limitation, legal fees and expenses, if this

Agreement is enforced against me. Due to the importance of this Agreement to the Employer, any claim I have against the Employer is a separate matter and does not entitled me to violate, or justify any violation of, this Agreement.

11. This Agreement shall be construed under the laws of the State of ____________________ without regard to its conflicts of laws principles. The only way this Agreement can be changed is in writing signed by both the Employer and me. Nothing in this Agreement shall be construed as a promise of employment or employment agreement. I acknowledge that I am and will be an "employee at will" of the Employer at all times, and that my employment with the Employer may be terminated at any time for any reason or no reason whatsoever.

Signature: _________________________________

Print Name: _________________________________

Address: _________________________________

Social Security Number:

____

ACKNOWLEDGED BY

_________________________________ (EMPLOYER)

By: _________________________________

Print Name and Title: _________________________________

FORM 4: OFFER OF EMPLOYMENT

_______________, 2____

____
____
____
____

Dear Mr./Mrs. ______________________:

We are pleased to offer you a full-time position with ______________________ ("Employer") as ______________________[title]. Specifics of our offer include:

1. You will be employed by Employer on a full-time basis subject to the terms of this letter commencing on ____, 2____, with annual performance reviews, and shall have the title of ______________________.

2. You will be compensated at an annual rate of $____, paid twice monthly on the fifteenth (15th) and the last day of each month, before withholding of federal and state income taxes, social security, unemployment insurance, and other customary deductions. [In addition, you will be paid up to an additional ____ % of your base salary as a combination of commission and bonus payments provided that you meet certain mutually agreed objectives, to be described in a separate letter between us.]

3. You will work a minimum of forty (40) hours per week with all requests for time off (other than holidays observed by all of Employer's employees) to be approved in advance by ______________________[name of immediate supervisor]. You will perform such tasks as shall be assigned

by ____________________[name of immediate supervisor] and such tasks as are usually and customarily performed by persons holding the title of ____________________.

4. You will be entitled to two (2) weeks' vacation, two (2) personal days and up to five (5) sick days, with pay. All vacation and personal days must be approved in advance by ____________________ [name of immediate supervisor]. You will also be entitled to the same paid holidays as are observed by all of Employer's employees.

5. You will be entitled to participate in Employer's medical insurance program and to such other employee benefits as Employer offers to all of its employees. You will be reimbursed for 100% of your reasonable and documented travel and living expenses incurred in the course of your employment, but any expense in excess of $____________________must be approved in advance by____________________ [name of immediate supervisor].

6. You will be employed on an "AT WILL" basis. That is, the terms of your employment shall continue unless terminated by either you or Employer. Termination by Employer may be with or without cause, at any time. The terminating party shall give the other party three working days notice prior to any termination. Employer reserves the right to pay the equivalent of three days of your salary in lieu of this notice requirement.

7. All work that you perform for Employer will be performed in our offices or as mutually agreed otherwise.

8. Your employment is to be considered exclusive to Employer. While you are employed by Employer, you will not perform services for compensation for any third party.

9. In consideration of your agreeing to this employment offer with Employer and as a condition of your reporting for work, we ask that you sign the attached "Noncompete and Nondisclosure Agreement" [see **Form 1** for a sample of this document].

10. This Agreement is governed by the laws of the State of ____________________.

If the terms of this offer are acceptable to you, please indicate below by signing and returning one copy of this letter to us, together with the signed "Noncompete and Nondisclosure Agreement." This offer is contingent upon a satisfactory check of your references.

Mr./Ms. ____________________, we are looking forward to having you join our company, and are sure that you will find your new career challenging and rewarding.

Sincerely,

[NAME OF COMPANY]

By:______________________________

Its ______________________________

ACCEPTED AND AGREED TO THIS ____

DAY OF ________, 2____:

Signature: ______________________________

Print Name: ______________________________

FORM 5: "EARN-IN" CLAUSE

Earn-In Arrangement for Member B. Not later than the 31st day of December in each calendar year during the term of this Agreement, Member A and Member B shall meet to review Member B's performance as an employee of the Company during such calendar year. Provided that such performance shall be at all times satisfactory to Member A in his reasonable discretion, and in consideration of services provided by Member B to the Company, the respective Membership Interests and Distribution Percentages of Member A and Member B shall be adjusted, without further act or instrument by the parties hereto, as follows:

(a) effective January 1, 2____ the Membership Interest and Distribution Percentage of Member B shall be X% and the Membership Interest and Distribution Percentage of Member A shall be Y%;

(b) effective January 1, 2____ the Membership Interest and Distribution Percentage of Member B shall be X + 2 % and the Membership Interest and Distribution Percentage of Member A shall be X – 2 %;

(c) effective January 1, 2____ the Membership Interest and Distribution Percentage of Member B shall be X + 4 % and the Membership Interest and Distribution Percentage of Member A shall be X – 4 %; and

(d) effective January 1, 2____ the Membership Interest and Distribution Percentage of Member B shall be X + 6 % and the Membership Interest and Distribution Percentage of Member A shall be X – 6 %;

provided that if Member A objects in writing to any adjustment contemplated by this Section _____ not later than the effective date of such adjustment, such adjustment shall not be effective and the respective Membership Interests and Distribution Percentages of Member A and Member B on the date of such writing shall remain in full force and effect until and unless otherwise mutually agreed by Member A and Member B.

FORM 6: "GOLDEN RULE" OR "RUSSIAN ROULETTE" BUYOUT CLAUSE

(a) The Members anticipate and intend that in managing the affairs of the Company, they will work closely with each other. Decisions generally will be made informally by consensus. The Members each agree to work with each other and to govern their actions by what each in good faith believes is in the best interest of the Company. In the event any Member (the "Offering Member") determines either (1) that the Members are so divided respecting the management of the Company's affairs that the votes required for action by the Members cannot be obtained, (2) that the Members are so divided that the votes required for the election of managers cannot be obtained, or (3) that there is internal dissension and two or more Members or factions of Members are so divided that dissolution would be beneficial to the Members, then and in such event the Offering Member may at any time offer, by written notice to the other Member or Members (the "Other Members"), to purchase the Membership Interests of the Other Members for a purchase price and upon such terms and conditions as the Offering Member may determine, subject to the provisions of this paragraph. Upon receipt of such written offer (the "Offering Member's Proposal"), the Other Members shall have thirty (30) days to accept or reject the Offering Member's Proposal by written notice delivered to the Offering Member. The failure to either accept or reject the Offering Member's Proposal in writing within such thirty (30) day period (the "Offer Period") shall constitute rejection of the Offering Member's Proposal. In the event the Other Members reject the Offering Member's Proposal, the Other Members shall have the right, pro rata, to purchase the Membership Interest of the Offering Member at the same purchase price and upon the same terms and conditions as are set forth

in the Offering Member's Proposal, by written notice delivered to the Offering Member within thirty (30) days after the earlier of (x) the expiration of the Offer Period and (y) the date of the Other Members' letter rejecting the Offering Member's Proposal.

(b) In the event the Offering Member's Proposal is rejected by the Other Members, and the Other Members fail to offer to purchase the Membership Interest of the Offering Member within ninety (90) days after receiving the Offering Member's Proposal, then the Company shall be dissolved in accordance with the Act.

(c) For purposes of this Section, the term "involuntary transfer" shall mean any transaction, proceeding or action by or in which a Member shall be deprived or divested of any right, title or interest in or to any of his Membership Interest (including, without limiting the generality of the foregoing, seizure under levy of attachment or execution, transfer in connection with bankruptcy or other court proceeding to a trustee in bankruptcy or receiver or other officer or agent, any transfer in the nature of equitable distribution or division of community property in a proceeding for divorce or marital separation, any transfer upon or occasioned by the dissolution, liquidation, incompetence or incapacity of a Member, or any transfer to a state or public officer, or agency pursuant to any statute pertaining to escheat or abandoned property).

FORM 7: "SUPERMAJORITY VOTING" CLAUSE

No act shall be taken, sum expended, decision made or obligation incurred by the Company except by the unanimous consent of all Members with respect to a matter within the scope of any of the following major decisions: (i) the sale of all or substantially all assets of the Company, (ii) the merger or consolidation of the Company with or into any other person or entity, (iii) the sale by any Member of a Majority in Interest of the Membership Interests of the Company, (iv) the dissolution, winding up, or liquidation of the business and affairs of the Company, (v) a mortgage or encumbrance upon all or substantially all assets of the Company, (vi) any matter which could result in a reduction of any Member's Percentage Interest in the Company, (vii) the Company's entering into any business or project other than as specifically set forth elsewhere in this Agreement, (viii) any change in the character of the business of the Company as set forth in this Agreement, (ix) the appointment of one or more managers to operate the business and affairs of the Company, (x) the disposal of the goodwill of the Company, (xi) any amendment, modification or termination of this Agreement or any Independent Contractor Agreement, (xii) the submission of any claim of the Company to arbitration, (xiii) the confession of a judgment, (xiv) the commission of any act which would make it impossible for the Company to carry on its ordinary business or (xv) the commission of any act, or the omission to take any act, that would contravene this Agreement.

FORM 8: "MANAGEMENT AND CONTROL" CLAUSE

Directors and Officers.

a. Each of the Stockholders agrees that so long as he shall remain a stockholder he will vote his respective shares of Stock in the Corporation for each of the following as a director so long as said director-designee remains a stockholder of the Corporation: [name directors]. Any of the foregoing directors who cease to be a stockholder of the Corporation shall simultaneously with the transfer or surrender of his shares submit to the Corporation his written resignation as director.

b. Each of the Stockholders agrees that so long as he shall remain a stockholder, he will cause the following persons to be appointed and elected an officer of the Corporation so long as the said officer-designee remains a Stockholder and proves faithful, efficient and competent:

As President: [name]

As Vice President: [name]

As Secretary: [name]

As Treasurer: [name]

Any of the foregoing officers who cease to be a stockholder of the Corporation shall simultaneously with the transfer or surrender of his shares submit to the Corporation his written resignation as officer.

ABOUT THE AUTHOR

Cliff Ennico (www.cliffennico.com), a nationally recognized authority on business start-ups, is best known as the host of *MoneyHunt*, the fast-paced PBS reality television series where entrepreneurs defend their business plans before America's toughest panel of experts. His weekly business advice column, Succeeding in Your Business, the "Ann Landers of the business world," is syndicated nationally by Creators Syndicate and appears in dozens of major newspapers and on small business Web sites throughout North America. He also writes for *Entrepreneur, Home Business Journal*, and other magazines, and hosts the "Protecting Your Business" channel for the Small Business Television Network at www.sbtv.com. A member of the faculty of eBay University (www.ebay.com/university), he delivers talks to business groups nationwide on the legal, tax, accounting, and human resources challenges of building a successful e-commerce company on eBay, the world's leading Internet auction site.

An attorney by training, Cliff has represented more than 5,000 small businesses in his twenty-five-year career and currently runs his own law practice in Fairfield, Connecticut. He has lectured on business and finance topics to business groups, venture capital clubs, and bar associations throughout the United States and has authored several leading books on small business law and management, including *MoneyHunt: 27 New Rules for Growing a Breakaway Business* (HarperCollins), *Forms for Small Business Entities* (Thomson/West), and *Basic Legal Forms* (Thomson/West). He holds a B.A. degree, magna cum laude, from Dartmouth College, and a law degree from Vanderbilt University, where he was Articles Editor of the *Vanderbilt Law Review*.

INDEX

J

K

L

M

N

O

P

R

S